ERIC RAVILIOUS

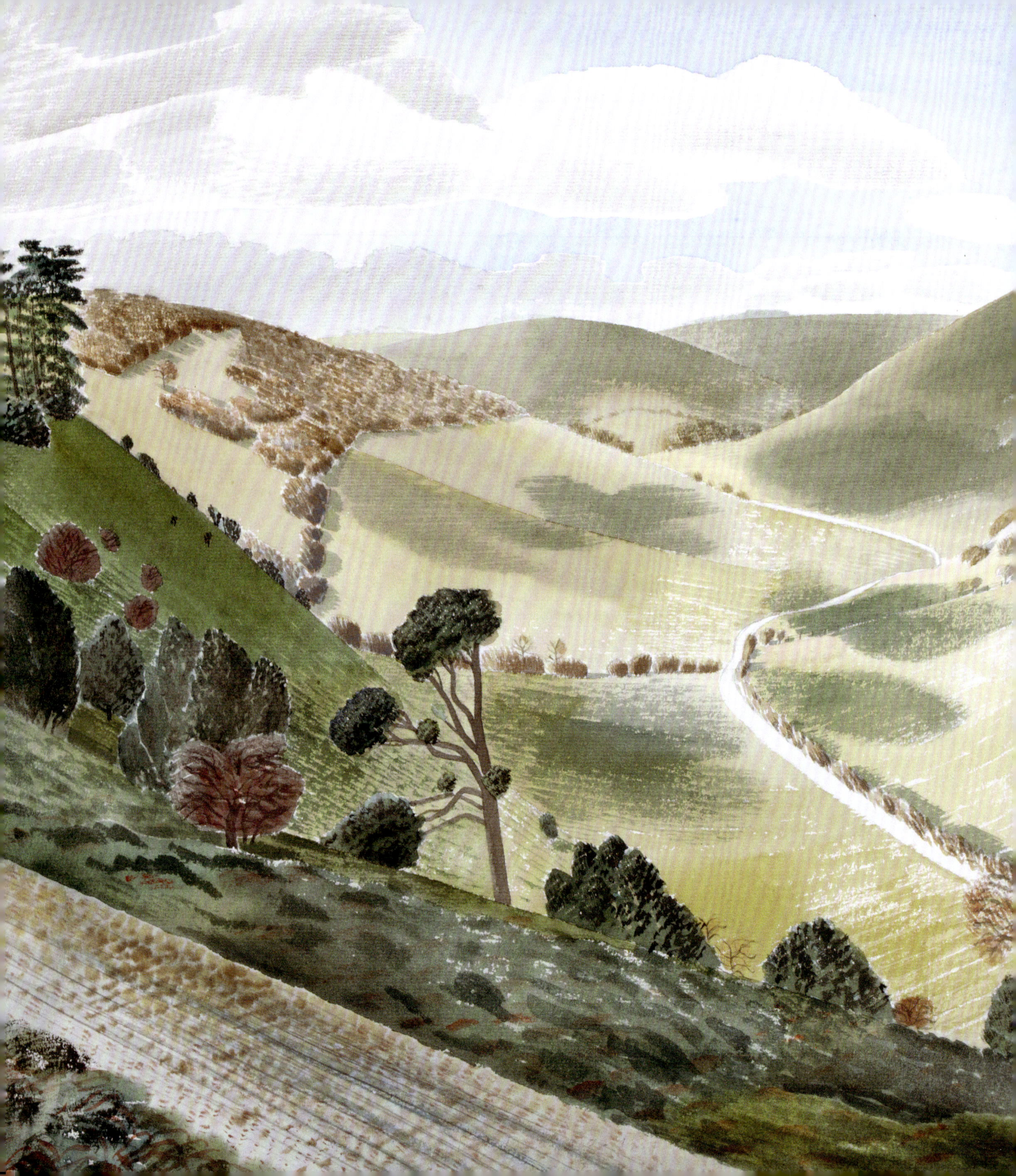

ERIC RAVILIOUS
DOWNLAND MAN

JAMES RUSSELL

WILTSHIRE MUSEUM
DEVIZES

PREFACE

The creation of an exhibition to celebrate Eric Ravilious and his love of the chalk downlands of southern England has been a long-held ambition. It was exciting to learn, having first discovered his work in the 1980s, of the importance of his watercolours inspired by the Wiltshire landscape, alongside his deep roots in Sussex. So the appearance at auction of his dummy for the *White Horse* Puffin book was an opportunity not to be missed.

For Wiltshire Museum it has been a long journey to our first major exhibition, bringing together loans from private lenders, regional galleries and national museums. We are grateful to have had the unwavering support of so many people and organizations. James Russell and Tim Mainstone helped at the very earliest stages with their enthusiasm. The support of the Oexmann family, alongside the ACE 'Ready to Borrow' programme, enabled us to create galleries that now meet national standards. Funding for the exhibition and the related engagement programme has come from the Weston Loan Programme with Art Fund and a range of other funders.

We have many people to thank for making the exhibition possible. I am deeply grateful to James Russell, our inspirational guest curator, and to our fantastic team at the Wiltshire Museum who have worked so hard to bring these amazing watercolours to Wiltshire. Thanks also to our enthusiastic team of volunteers and for the unstinting support of our Trustees. Special thanks are due to Lucy Morton, who designed this stunning catalogue, and Julian Francis for his generous sponsorship of the catalogue.

DAVID DAWSON, DIRECTOR, WILTSHIRE MUSEUM

PREVIOUS SPREAD
The Causeway, Wiltshire Downs, detail.

OPPOSITE
White Horse, cover of dummy for proposed Puffin book, 1939–40.

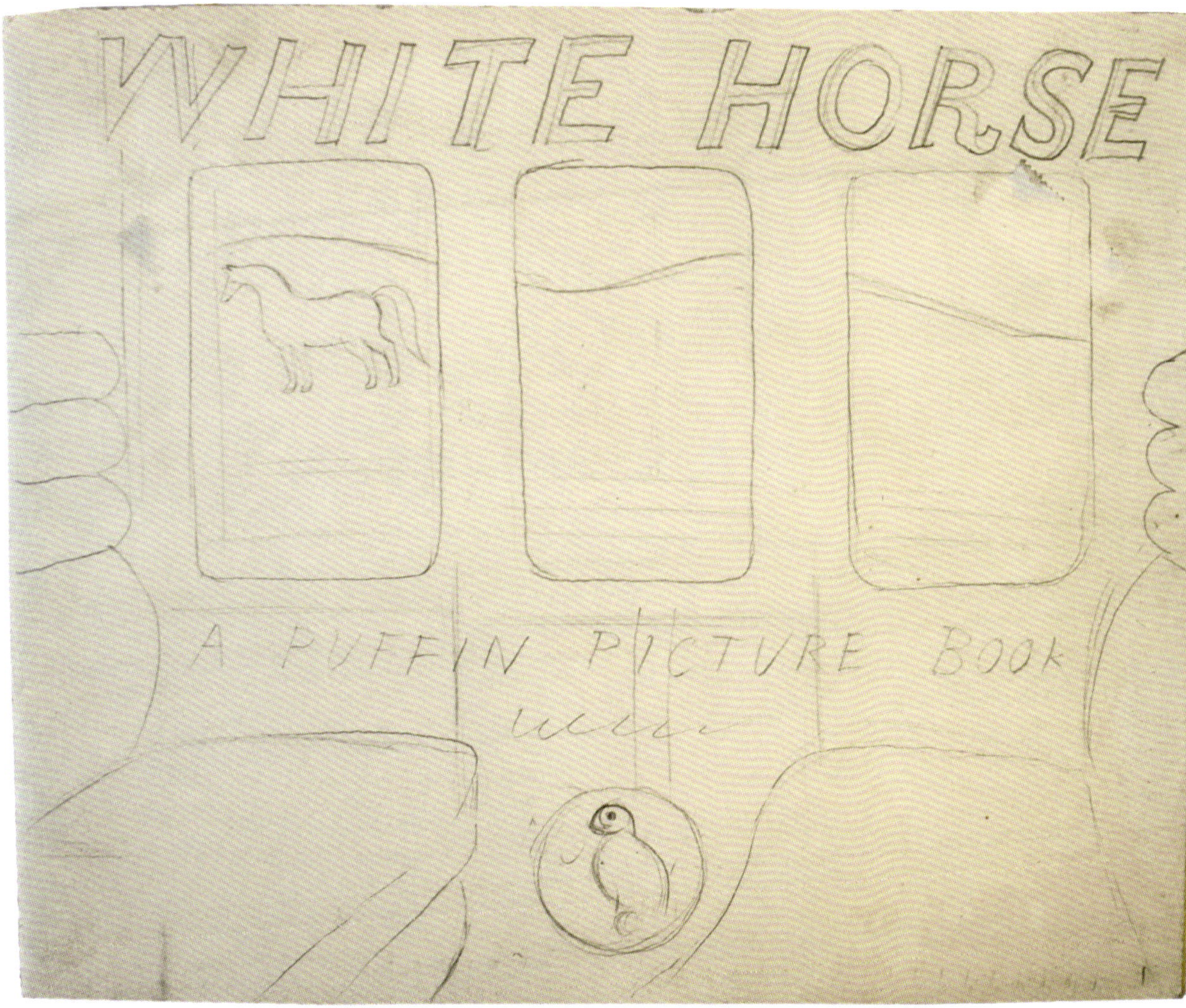
WHITE HORSE
A PUFFIN PICTURE BOOK

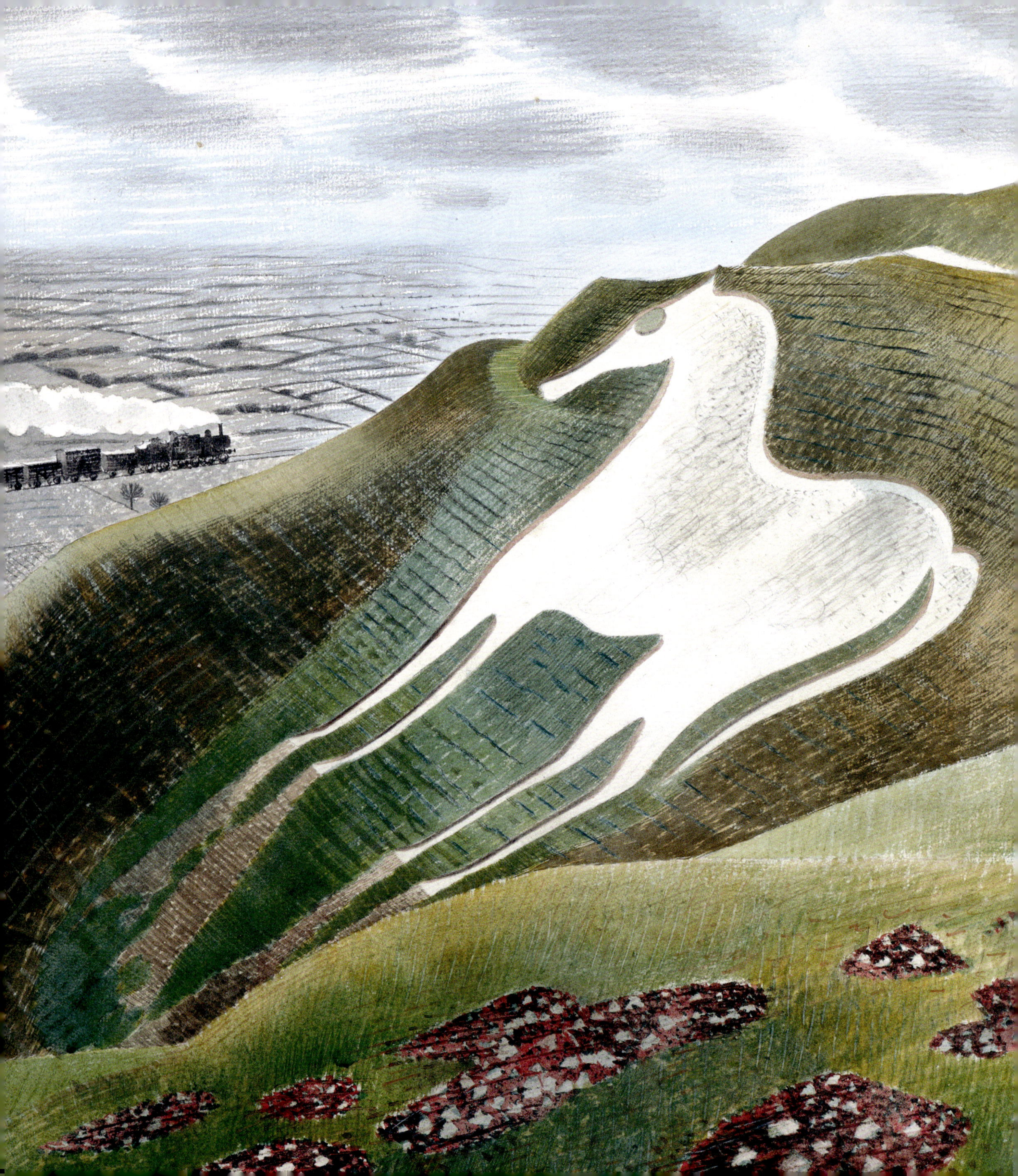

DOWNLAND MAN

> The long white roads … are a temptation. What quests they propose! They take us away to the thin air of the future or the underworld of the past.
>
> Edward Thomas, *The South Country*

In 2012 an auction held by Sworders of Essex featured an unusual lot: a few sheets of paper bound together to form a slim booklet, with a cover roughly drawn in pencil and the title *White Horse*. To most people this must have seemed a very odd thing to covet, yet Lot 345 was deemed worthy of a mention in the *New York Times*, which described the booklet as the rough draught of a children's picture book – a 'dummy' to industry insiders. It had been put together by British designer and watercolourist Eric Ravilious (1903–1942) and sent to Noel Carrington, publisher of Penguin's series of Puffin Picture Books. It had apparently then vanished. Carrington suggested that the artist had taken it to Iceland in August 1942 and perhaps carried it with him early the following month, on the flight from which he never returned.

Yet here the dummy was. Inside were black-and-white photographs of Ravilious watercolours such as *The Westbury Horse*, with scribbled lines denoting text. The cover meanwhile featured a design based on the watercolour *Train Landscape*, with the Puffin symbol in the space usually occupied by the figure 3, denoting Third Class. The prediction among Ravilious watchers was that a private collector – either a diehard Rav fan or, possibly, a Penguin Books enthusiast – would end up with this ephemeral treasure. When the dust settled

The Westbury Horse, detail.

it came as a surprise to discover that the successful bidder, acting on behalf of the Wiltshire Museum, was David Dawson – the Museum's director.

'We just decided we had to have this', David told the *New York Times*, and when I went to Devizes to view the dummy I began to understand why. I already knew that the downland landscapes of southern England had inspired Ravilious more than any other, but now I could see that his work might in turn be valued by the twenty-first-century champions of those landscapes and their varied histories. Talking to David, I realized that the relationship between Ravilious and the Downs was more complicated and intriguing than I had previously thought. For one thing, his personal interest in the chalk hills and their history echoed a contemporary obsession with the subject. For another, Ravilious explored these hills so often and in such a variety of ways that his work serves as a marvellous, imaginative appendix to the surveys conducted by antiquarians like William Stukeley, Richard Colt-Hoare and myriad others whose books are kept in the Museum's library.

Ravilious was born in London in 1903 but in boyhood moved with his family to a settlement being built at Hampden Park, north of Eastbourne, Sussex. To the east lay the railway; to the west open country led to the foot of the Downs a couple of miles away. In this idyllic setting Ravilious enjoyed childhood games and endured the family's relentless chapel-going. He had a sunny, somewhat mischievous disposition, and from the earliest age an almost miraculous talent for drawing. While still a boy he could making a drawing of a boot that didn't just resemble a boot; it brought the boot to life.

This skill in drawing took him to the Eastbourne School of Art and then to the Royal College of Art, which in those days had a connecting door to the Victoria and Albert Museum. By his late teens he was studying Alfred Rich's well-known watercolour primer, which encouraged students to explore landscape in the company of pre-Victorian artists like John Robert Cozens and John Sell Cotman. Once in London he was able to study, in the print rooms of the V&A and the British Museum, the work of these and numerous other watercolourists of that golden age. In the summer holidays he went sketching around Sussex, focusing at first on traditional romantic subjects: quaint old streets, tumbledown buildings and even a castle.

Sussex Church, wood engraving, 1925.

But the watercolour he sold at the Royal College's 1923 Sketch Club exhibition is different.

Wannock Dew Pond has been rather studiously painted, in sombre tones, but there is not a ruin in sight. We are up on the Downs, only a short (if arduous) bike ride from the artist's boyhood home and at first glance the hills seem featureless. Look closely, though, and you'll see a small, pale cigar shape in the dun-coloured grass. This is the dew pond of the title, more accurately 'rain pond', dug in the porous chalk to provide drinking water for sheep. Such ponds were still being dug and maintained when Ravilious first went exploring the Downs, so this is contemporary rural life we're looking at, not an ancient monument. In fact, there are prehistoric earthworks and tumuli all around this spot, but Ravilious picked for his subject a place where the turf had been cut away, the chalk revealed.

What was it about this scene that appealed to him so strongly? He had been exploring the Downs since boyhood, and by this time had read Gilbert White of Selborne and Edward Thomas, for whom the chalk hills were synonymous with freedom. Unlike most Londoners who read these books, he had intimate first-hand knowledge of the chalk hills, gained not only by cycling to local villages like Alfriston but also on longer excursions. The summer before he enrolled at the Royal College, he and a couple of friends walked for a week or more along lanes Thomas might have known, through a human landscape of small farms and crumbling manor houses. So maybe he chose the dew pond in part because it was a subject nobody else knew about. Then again, Ravilious was also a budding wood engraver. Perhaps the idea of a pond 'engraved' into the chalk appealed to him.

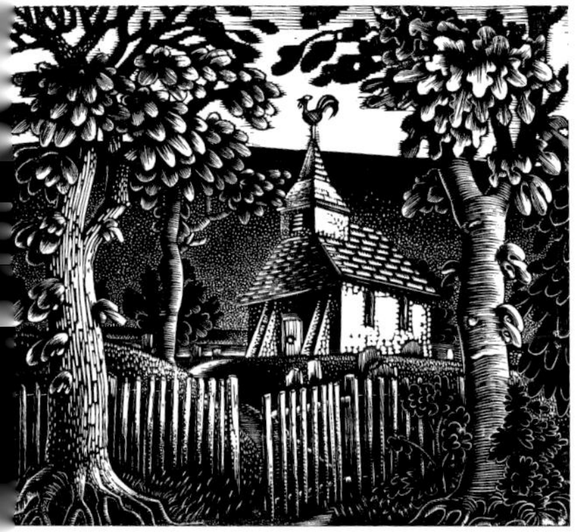

No doubt the dew pond attracted him on many levels, but the unusual nature of the subject was certainly important because even as a student originality mattered greatly to Ravilious. When he began studying wood engraving he first made the decision to become a white-line engraver, using the medium to create a white-on-black image. Through the nineteenth century wood engraving had chiefly been used to create black-on-white images, in order to replicate drawings, but a movement had begun during the Edwardian period to bring back white-line engraving as practised by the great Thomas Bewick. Artists like

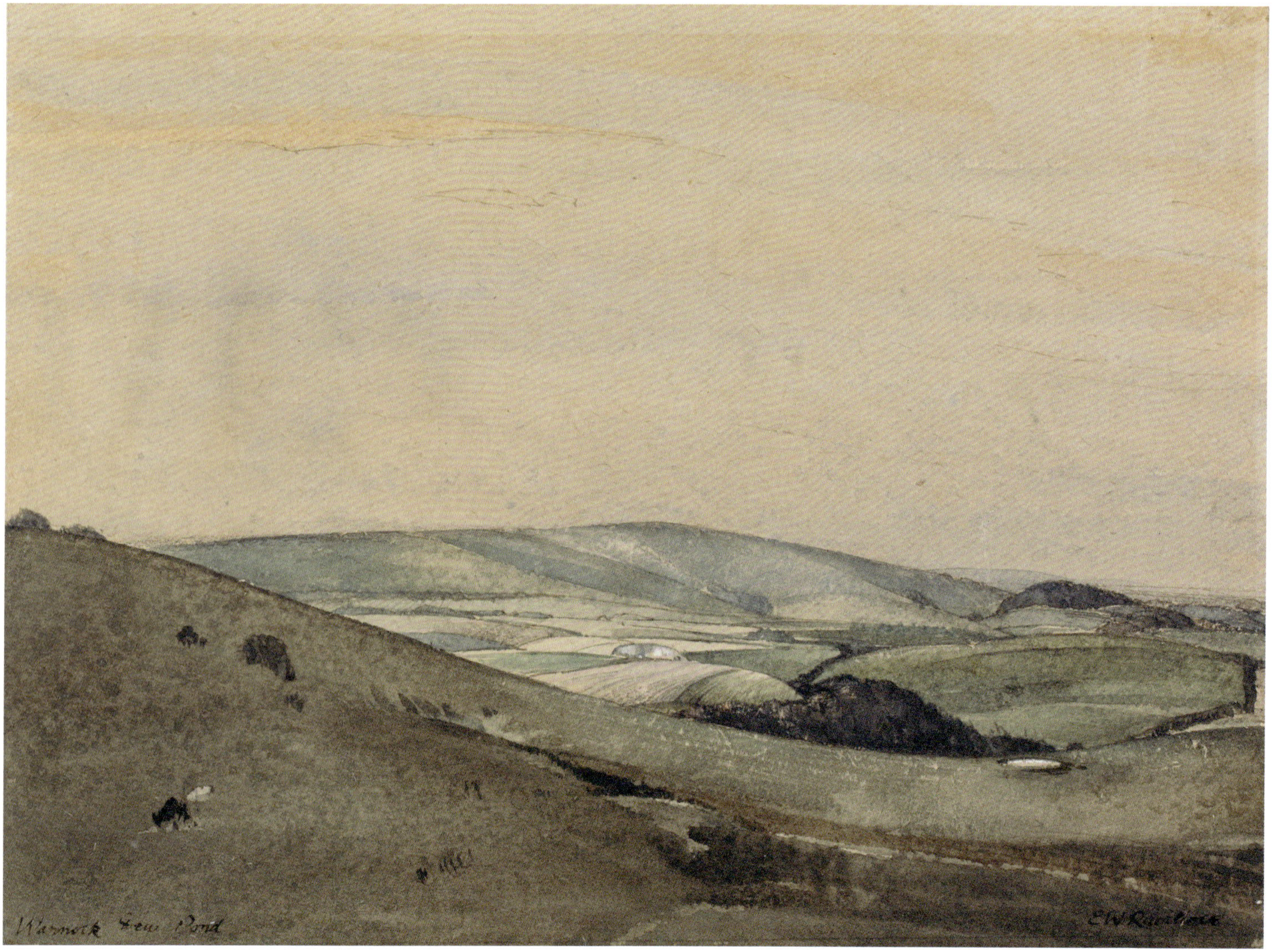

WANNOCK DEW POND

1923, watercolour, pen and brown ink, 27.8 × 38.6 cm, British Museum

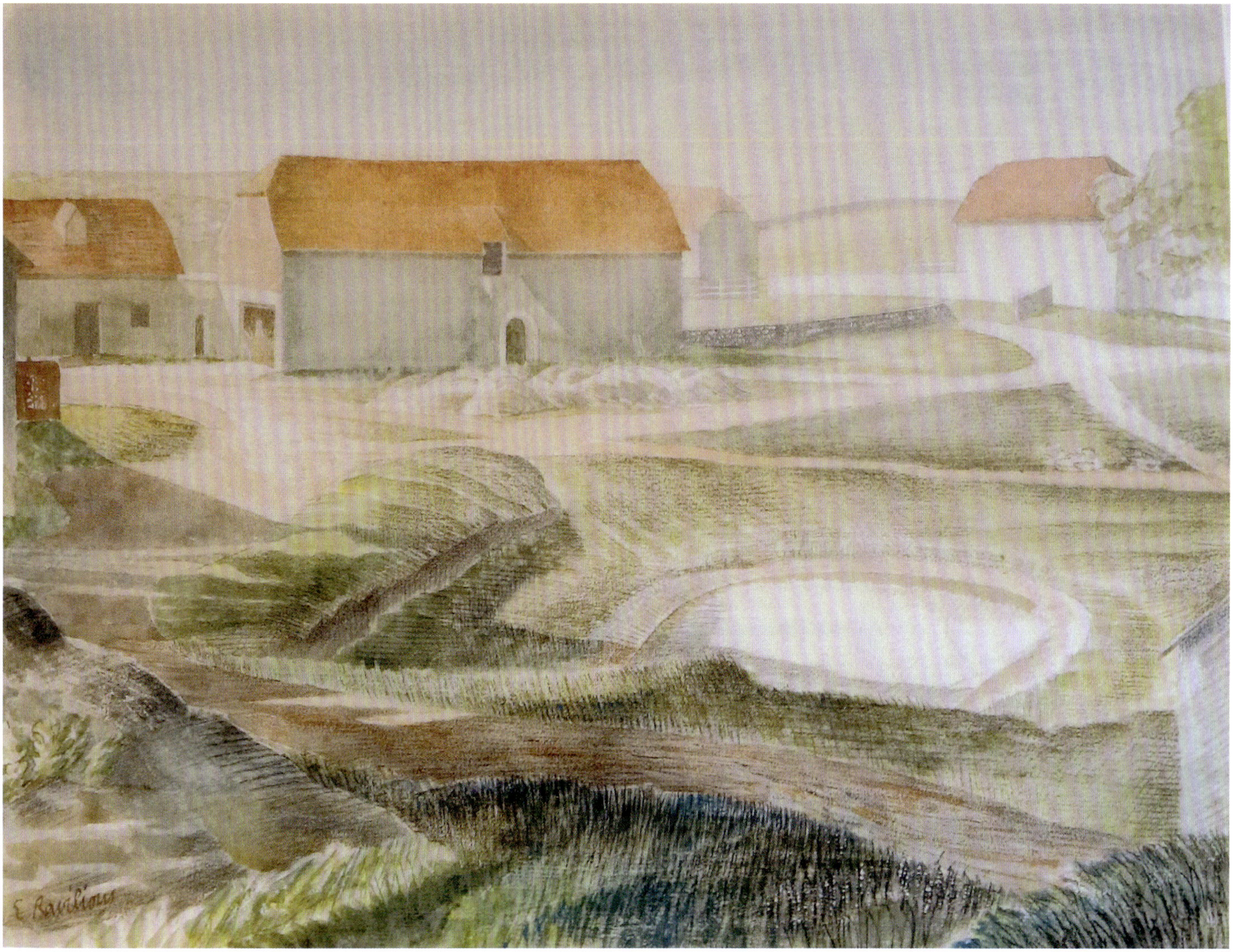

POND AT BIRLING MANOR FARM (EAST DEAN)

1925, watercolour and pencil, 29 × 38.5 cm, Towner, Eastbourne

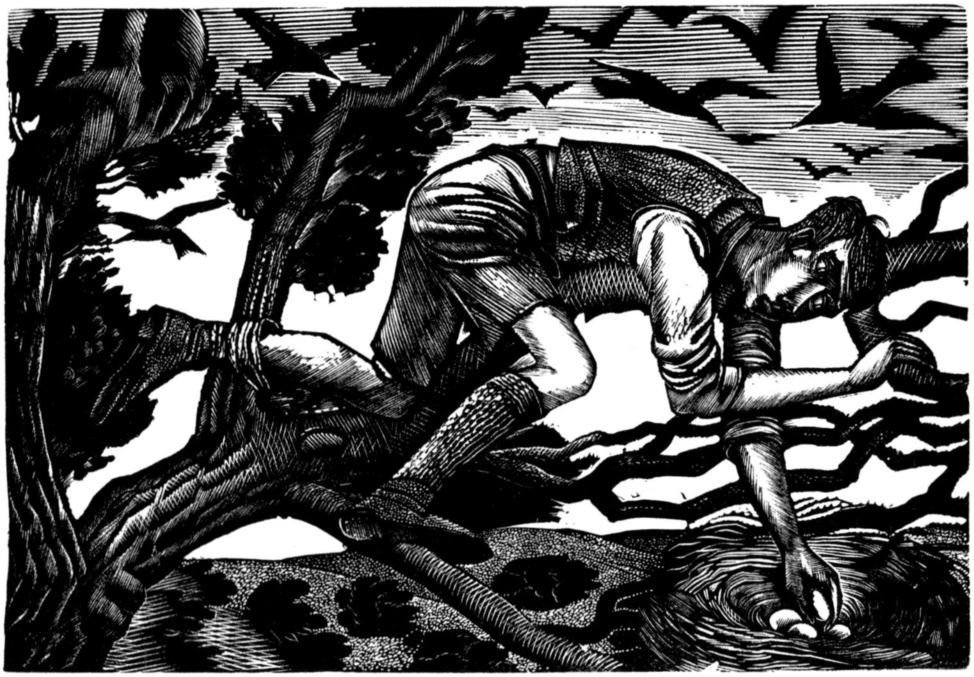

Boy Birdnesting, wood engraving, 1927.

Gwen Raverat and the brothers Paul and John Nash led the way, but Ravilious didn't just follow. He went a step further, learning medieval printmaking techniques that allowed him to introduce pattern into his engravings, and devising his own tools to do so.

You can see in engravings like *Boy Birdnesting* and *Sussex Church* how he used this approach to portray the textures of tree bark, clothing and land, and so create decorative, atmospheric worlds that were unlike anyone else's. This method particularly suited downland subjects as the glimmer of white through black mimicked the appearance of chalk grassland. Soon his work was appearing in fine press books, and in trade publications like the *Lanston Monotype Almanack* of 1929. An edition of this diary-cum-reference work was produced every year by the London office of the famous American type company, as a gift for its clients, and it was a sign of the artist's growing reputation that he was asked to contribute a set of wood engravings that year.

For the *Almanack* he brought zodiacal beings into the familiar landscape of Sussex, using the play of black and white to dramatic effect and introducing chalk figures both imaginary (Aries) and real. In the engraving of Taurus he introduced a figure well known to regular travellers between Brighton and Eastbourne. Usually known as the Long Man of Wilmington, this giant is of uncertain age and origin, being neither demonstrably ancient nor of a known modern date, and to Ravilious it was also of uncertain gender. In fact, he was convinced that the figure depicted was female, and so portrayed here a giantess with rounded hips. At her feet lies a dew pond in which a constellation of stars is reflected, and beside that stands a sign. Here, in miniature, is Ravilious's interpretation of downland, a place at once dreamlike and prosaic – where real life and imagination meet.

The Wilmington chalk figure must have preoccupied Ravilious considerably in the late 1920s as it features again in the set of murals he painted alongside Edward Bawden at Morley College in Lambeth, London. Much admired at the time, the murals were destroyed by enemy action during the war, leaving us

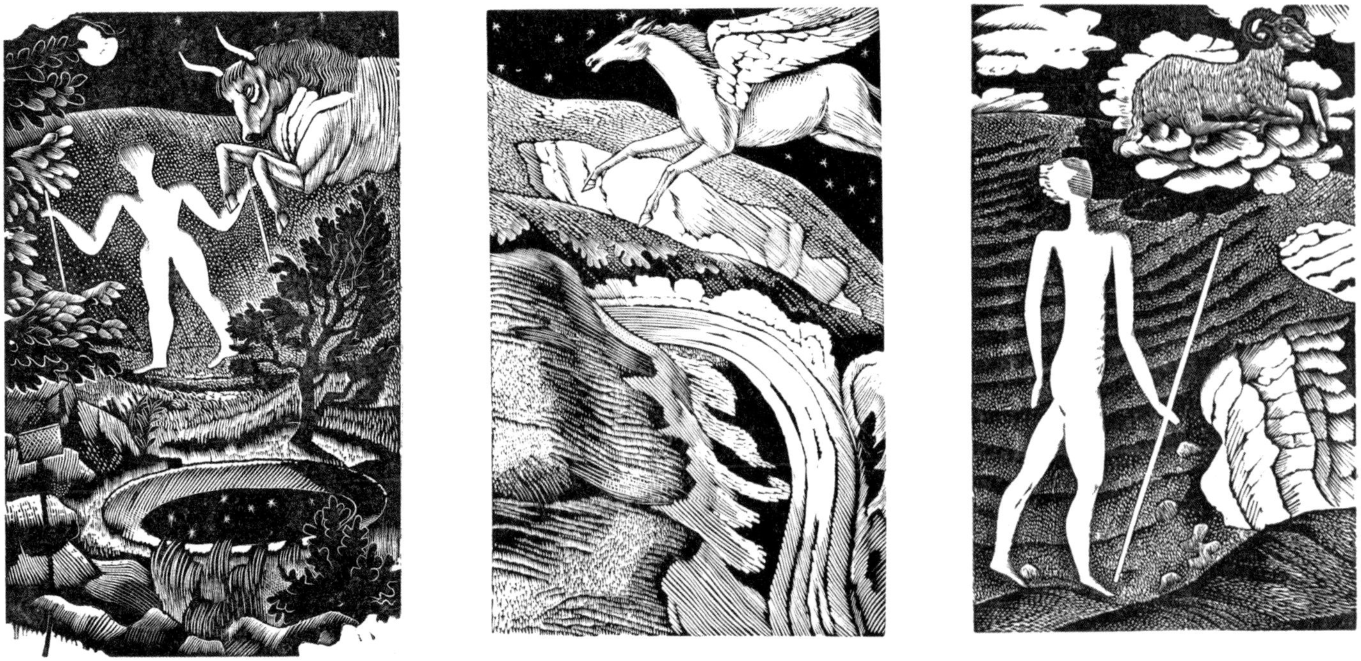

Taurus, *Pegasus* and *Aries*, wood engravings, 1929.

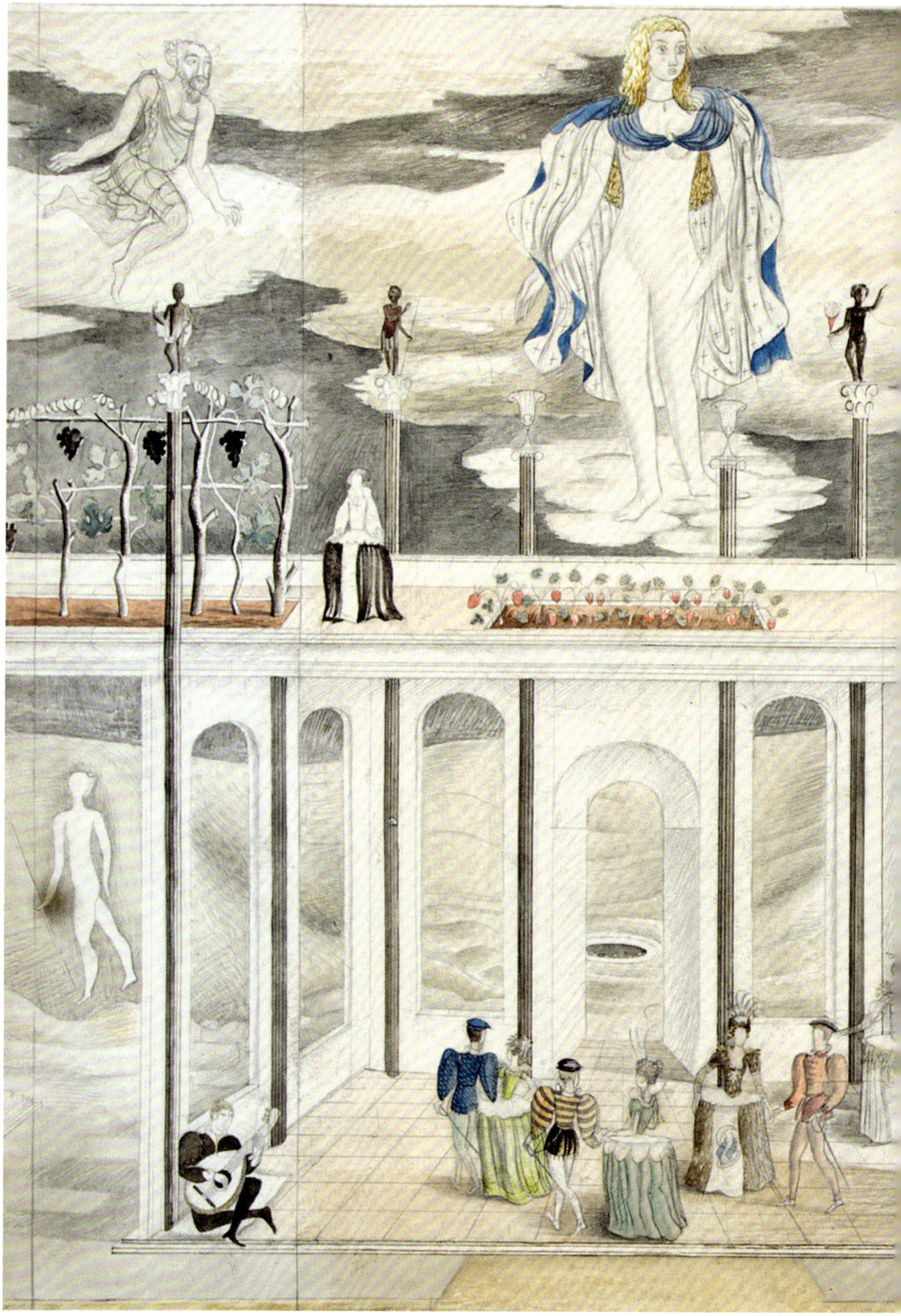

STUDY FOR MORLEY COLLEGE MURALS

1928–30, watercolour and pencil, 47 × 81 cm, private collection

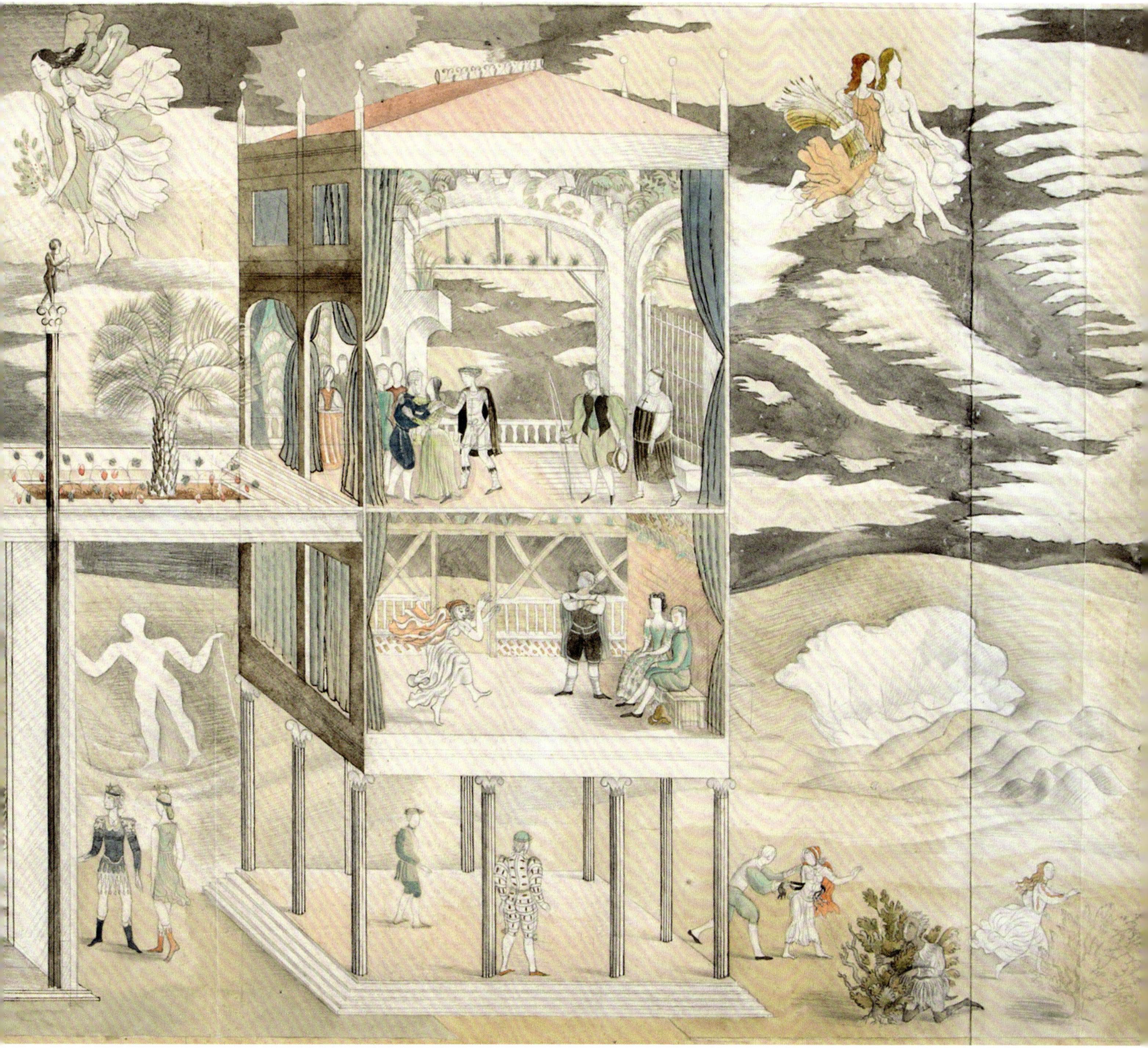

only photographs to remember them by, along with studies such as the one included here. The scheme was designed to celebrate Elizabethan and Jacobean theatre, with scenes from numerous plays enacted in whimsical, open-sided pavilions. Above are flying figures like those on the walls of Pompeii, while the landscape serving as a backdrop to the action is a simplified version of downland, with the Wilmington Giant a powerful presence beyond the pillared porticos.

Curiously, it took Ravilious many years to approach this or any other chalk figure as a fine artist. When asked to exhibit watercolours alongside work by Edward Bawden and Douglas Percy Bliss at the St George Gallery in London, he turned to the chalk hills for subject matter, but focused (so far as we can tell from surviving works) on inhabited places. Birling Manor Farm, East Dean he visited more than once, creating two known watercolours that focus on the newly dug pond in the farmyard. The farm itself may have offered a study in old Sussex vernacular, but the pond is new and raw. *Litlington, Sussex* shows his willingness to work with a dry brush, allowing the whiteness of paper to shine through (a technique learned from Paul Nash, who found it in Cézanne's watercolours), but in *Firle Beacon* we begin to see the Ravilious vision emerging most clearly. While the foliage and clouds are wildly animated (Nash again), the fence is almost a quotation from John Sell Cotman. But there's a desire to set the eye in motion from foreground to distance, so conjuring a slightly unsettling feeling of contained space, which is all Ravilious.

Much of this focus on the Downs had come about because Ravilious was back in Eastbourne, staying with his parents and teaching at the art school. But by the end of the decade he had left and it wasn't until 1934 that he found his way back to the Sussex Downs. In the interim he had married Tirzah Garwood, a former student, and moved to a flat near the Thames in Hammersmith. In between teaching at the Royal College and undertaking design commissions he devoted himself to watercolour painting, making the most of opportunities such as a 1932 invitation to stay at Oare House, near Pewsey. He had met the owner, Sir Geoffrey Fry, at the opening of the Morley College murals a couple of years earlier, and Sir Geoffrey proved to be both a source of encouragement and a valuable patron. Ravilious would return to Wiltshire on several occasions during the following decade, sometimes staying at Oare House and sometimes with fellow artist John Nash (who lived in Meadle, Bucks).

With Sir Geoffrey Fry's help Ravilious's first solo exhibition achieved good sales, and the following year he was invited by Peggy Angus, an old friend from the Royal College, to stay at her cottage in the South Downs. Called Furlongs, and sited on a track that runs along the base of Beddingham Hill near Glynde, this humble but attractive flint-faced house is today a site of pilgrimage for Ravilious fans. Walking past and up the hill the scene seems as empty and still as a Ravilious watercolour, but we should be wary of assuming that the landscape was so quiet then. In fact when Angus found the cottage it was divided into two, and she shared a scullery with her neighbour, a ploughman named Barnes who was employed by the Glynde Estate to work at the farm behind the cottage. All year round, in all weathers, Barnes worked the land with his horses and men, and it is the roller he used that stands in the foreground of *Downs in Winter*.

Angus was a struggling painter who would in later life become a celebrated designer of tiles and wallpapers. She taught art in order to pay the bills and in this professional capacity visited the Soviet Union in 1930, returning home an impassioned convert to Communism. Nicknamed the Red Angus for her bullish temperament as much as for as her political views (not to mention her Scottishness), she proselytized constantly and in her own painting sought to emulate the realist style of Soviet art. She painted portraits of agricultural workers, and in the spring of 1934 led Ravilious up Beddingham Hill to the chalk quarry and cement works that had engulfed Virginia Woolf's house Asheham a decade earlier.

The Asham Cement Works was seen by most well-meaning people as a blot on the landscape, yet it inspired Ravilious to produce a number of works. Indeed, there are few peacetime locations he explored in such detail, but what was it he found so stimulating about this industrial landscape? He was certainly attracted to the strangeness of the scene, with its chalk-whitened buildings and landscape dusted with fine white chalk. At the same time there were echoes in the quarry's topography of the Alpine scenery painted by eighteenth-century watercolourists like Francis Towne, but this landscape was on a human scale and of course man-made – being made even as the artists watched. This was a twentieth-century scene, the product of a twentieth-century need for building materials.

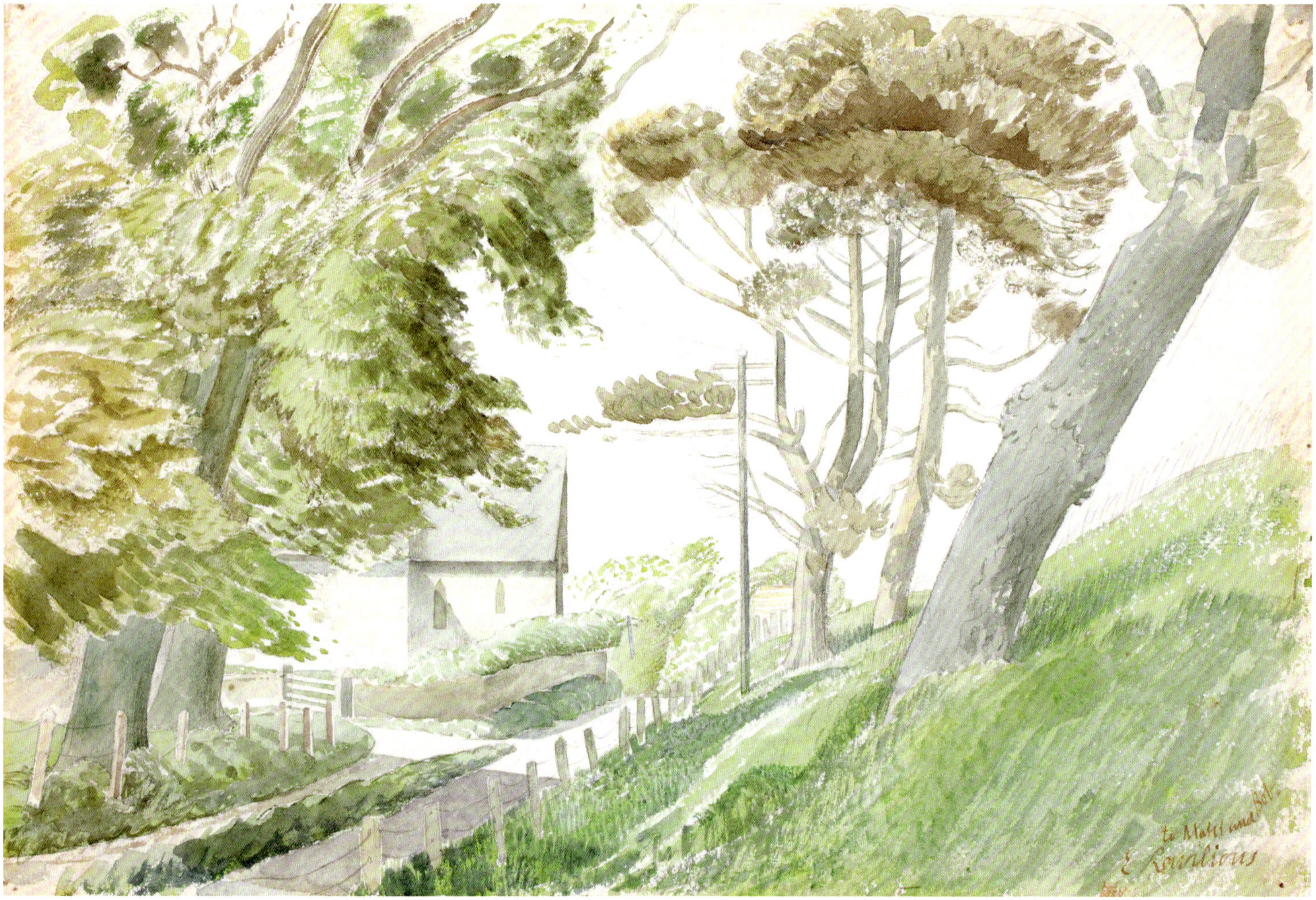

LITLINGTON, SUSSEX

c.1920, watercolour, ink and pencil, 25.2 × 36.7 cm, Towner, Eastbourne

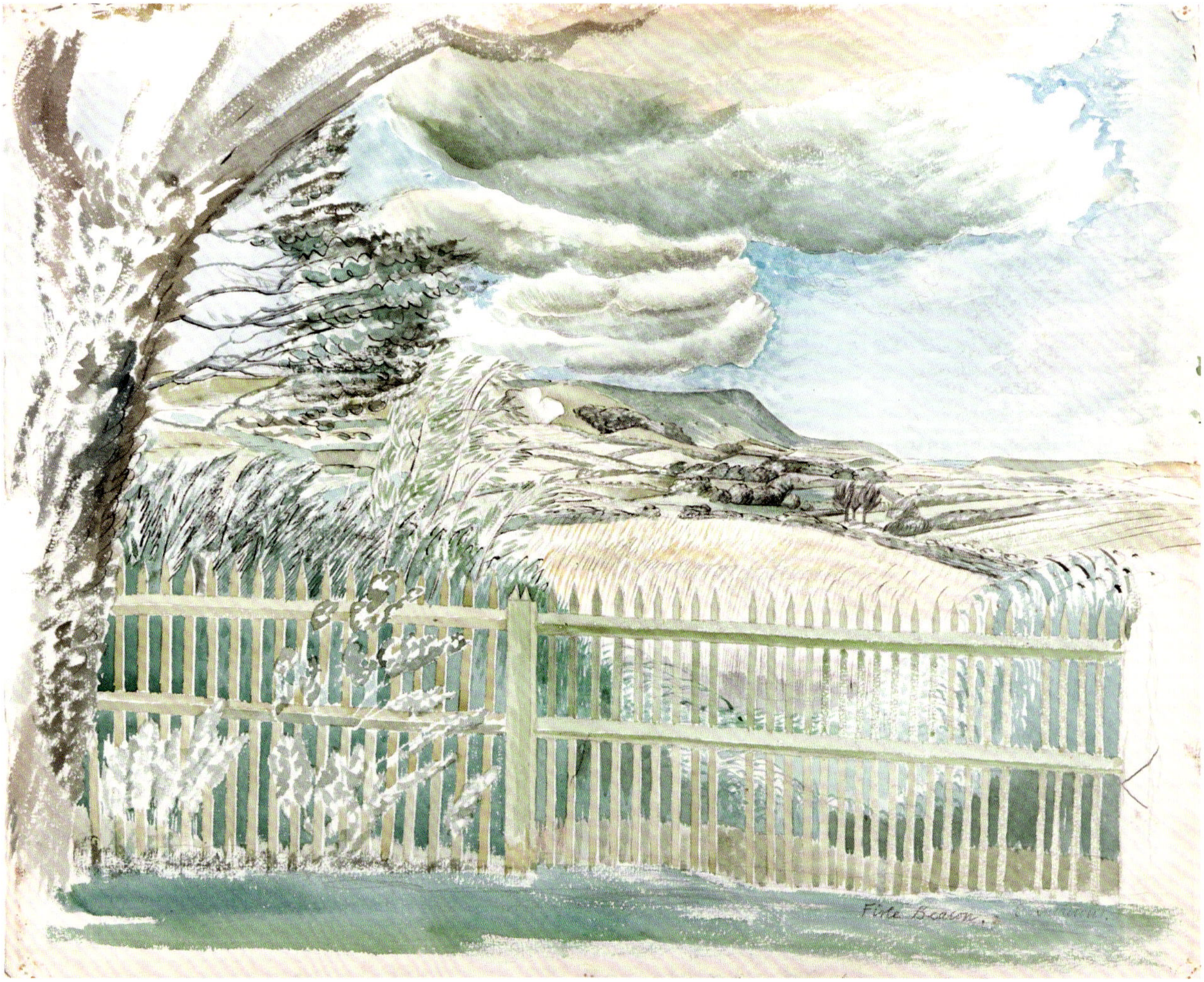

FIRLE BEACON

1927, watercolour, pen and pencil, 40 × 49.5 cm, Amgueddfa Cymru – National Museum Wales

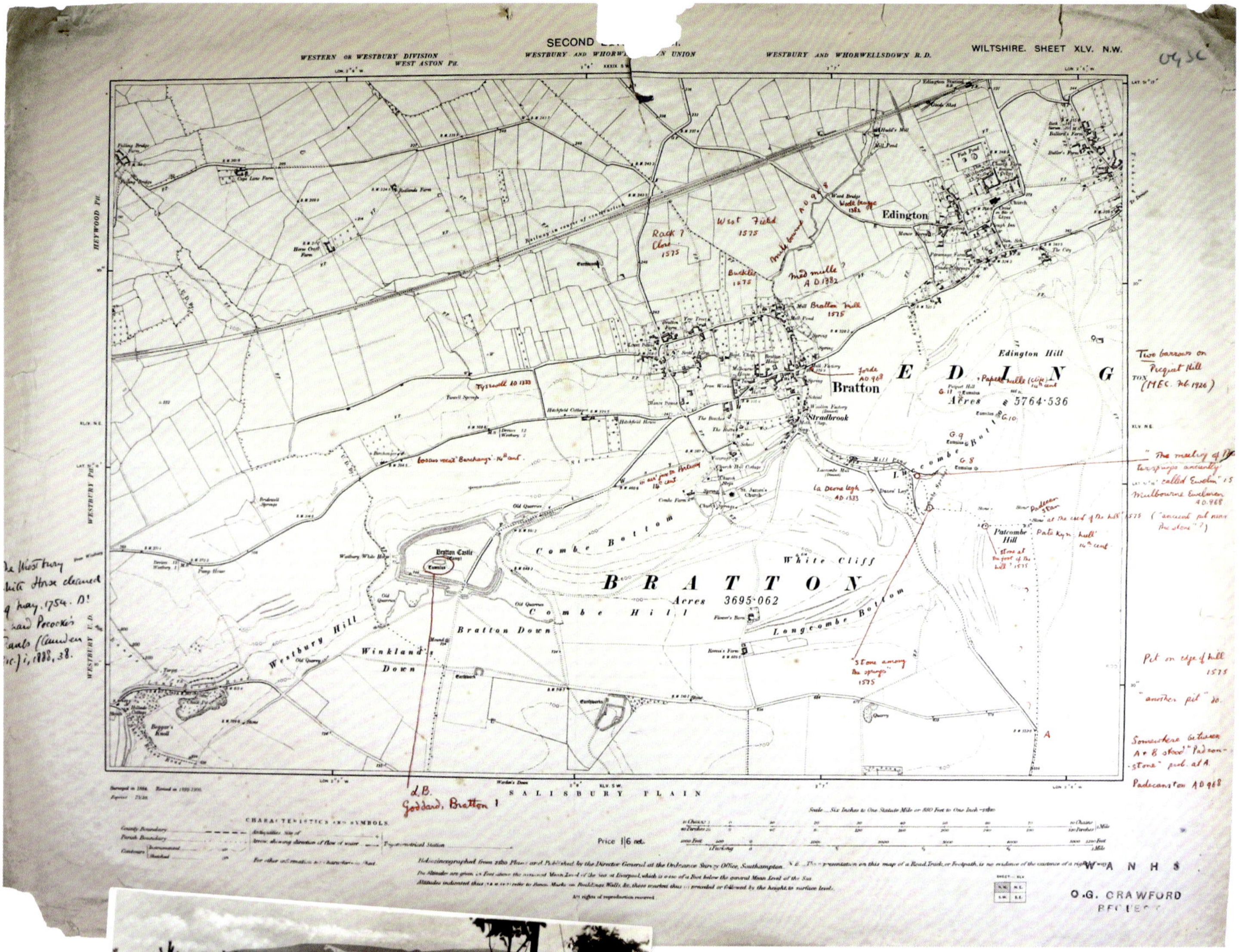
WILTSHIRE. SHEET XLV. N.W.
WESTERN OR WESTBURY DIVISION
WEST ASTON Pℓ.
WESTBURY AND WHORWELLSDOWN R.D.
Edington
Bratton
Stradbrook
Edington Hill
EDING
Acres 5764·536
BRATTON
Acres 3695·062
Bratton Castle
Westbury White Horse
Combe Bottom
Combe Hill
White Cliff
Bratton Down
Westbury Hill
Winkland's Down
Longcombe Bottom
Patcombe Hill
SALISBURY PLAIN
HEYWOOD Pℓ.
WESTBURY Pℓ.
Price 1/6 net.
CHARACTERISTICS AND SYMBOLS.
O.G. CRAWFORD
W A N H S
West Field 1575
Bratton Mille 1575
Tysseswell AD 1333
Forde AD 968
Two barrows on Picquet Hill
Pit on edge of hill 1575
"another pit" do.
Padecanston AD 968
"Stone among the springs" 1575
Goddard, Bratton

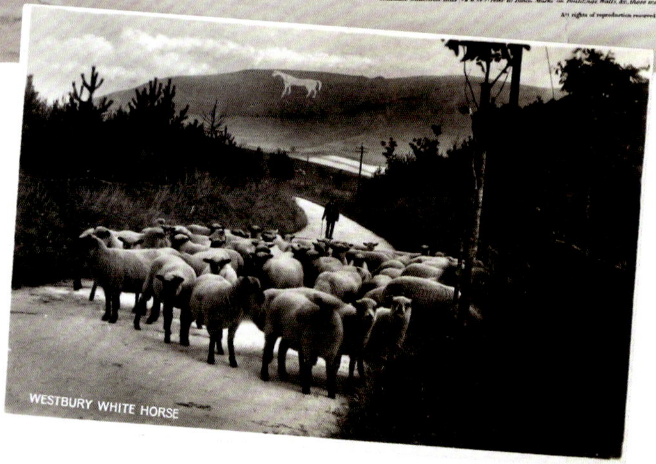
WESTBURY WHITE HORSE

Ordnance survey map, 1901, Wiltshire Sheet XLV NW, showing Bratton, annotated by O.G.S. Crawford.

Postcard showing Westbury Horse, c.1920s.

Elsewhere in southern England excavations of a very different kind were under way. Between the wars around forty Iron Age hill forts were excavated by archaeologists as the nation was gripped by a mania for prehistory. This had its roots in the nineteenth century, when the spreading railway network allowed the curious to travel with ease around the country and every county had detailed guidebooks listing local antiquities and museums filled with unearthed treasures. Writing at the turn of the twentieth century, author Edward Thomas described his journeys along supposedly ancient downland routes like the Icknield Way, while Londoners responded to advertising posters that encouraged them to take day trips into the Chilterns. Young urbanites lost themselves in the world described by mystic Arthur Machen in his semi-autobiographical novel *The Hill of Dreams* (1907), in which a boy exploring the earthworks of a Roman fort experiences strange fantasies and at one point time-travels back to see the place as a living settlement. In Edwardian London the book acquired cult status. Among the young people who absorbed its ideas was Paul Nash, an artist whose main preoccupation remained throughout his life the power of place.

In 1912 Nash had a Machen-like moment of heightened awareness overlooking the twin hills known as the Wittenham Clumps. Rising side by side from the flat Thames Valley, each topped with a dense stand of beeches, the hills were, he said, the pyramids of his small world – mysterious and distinctive and charged with the history of human habitation extending back to the Bronze Age. The reference to pyramids reminds us of the excitement engendered worldwide by the gradual uncovering of Egypt's ancient past, which reached fever pitch with the discovery of Tutankhamun's tomb in 1922.

Back in Britain, the 1920s saw an ever-deepening fascination with prehistory. A notable pioneer was O.G.S. Crawford, an archaeologist appointed to the Ordnance Survey with the enviable task of updating the prehistoric content on the Survey's maps. Everyday fieldwork he conducted by bicycle, but, having served as an airman during the Great War, he also understood the value of aerial photography and used RAF photographs to help him in his work. This innovation appealed to archaeologist (and marmalade millionaire) Alexander Keiller, who had coincidentally used aerial photos while working for military intelligence during the war. He paid for the pair of them to conduct a systematic

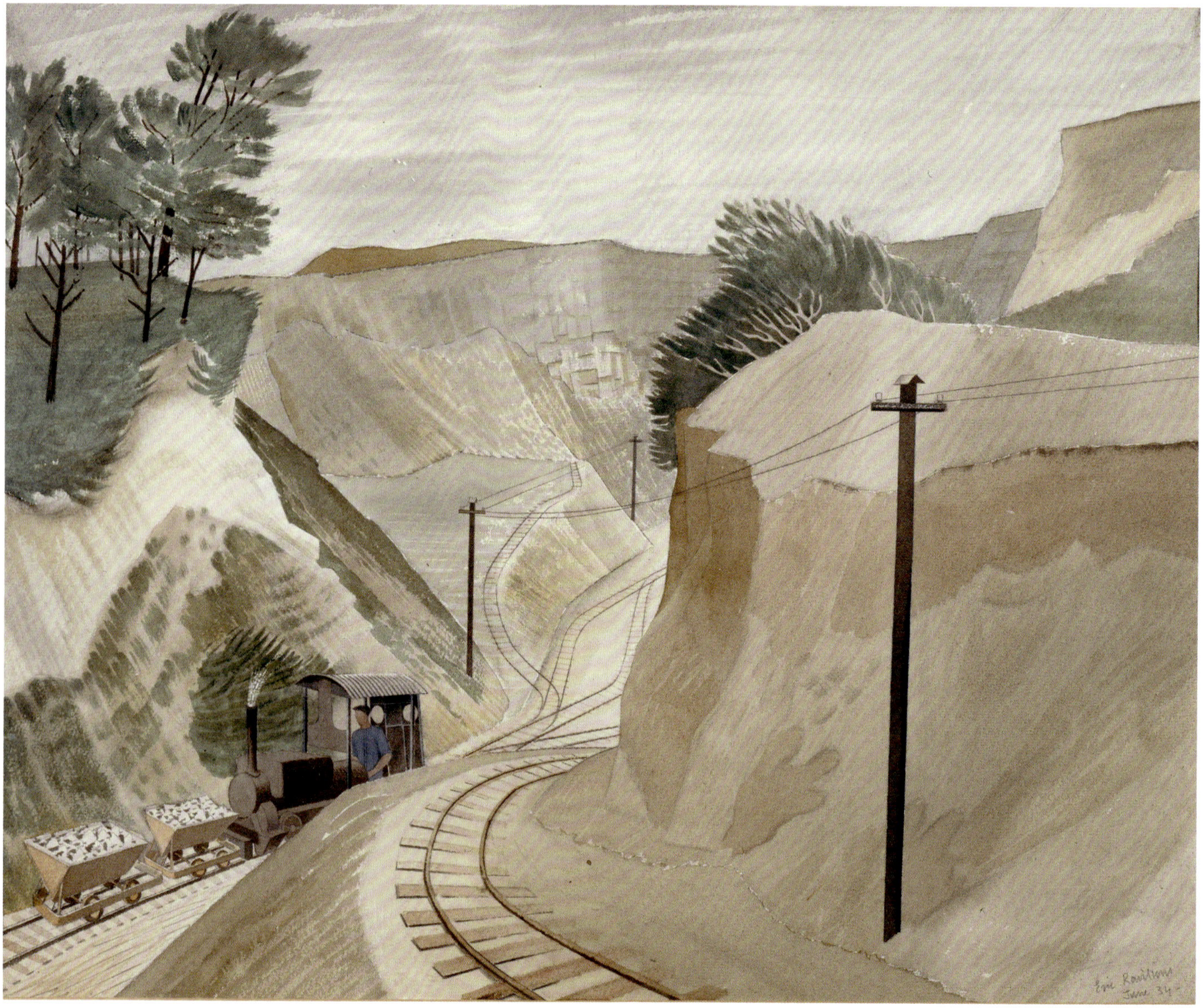

THE CEMENT PIT

1934, watercolour and pencil, 44.4 × 55.8 cm, private collection

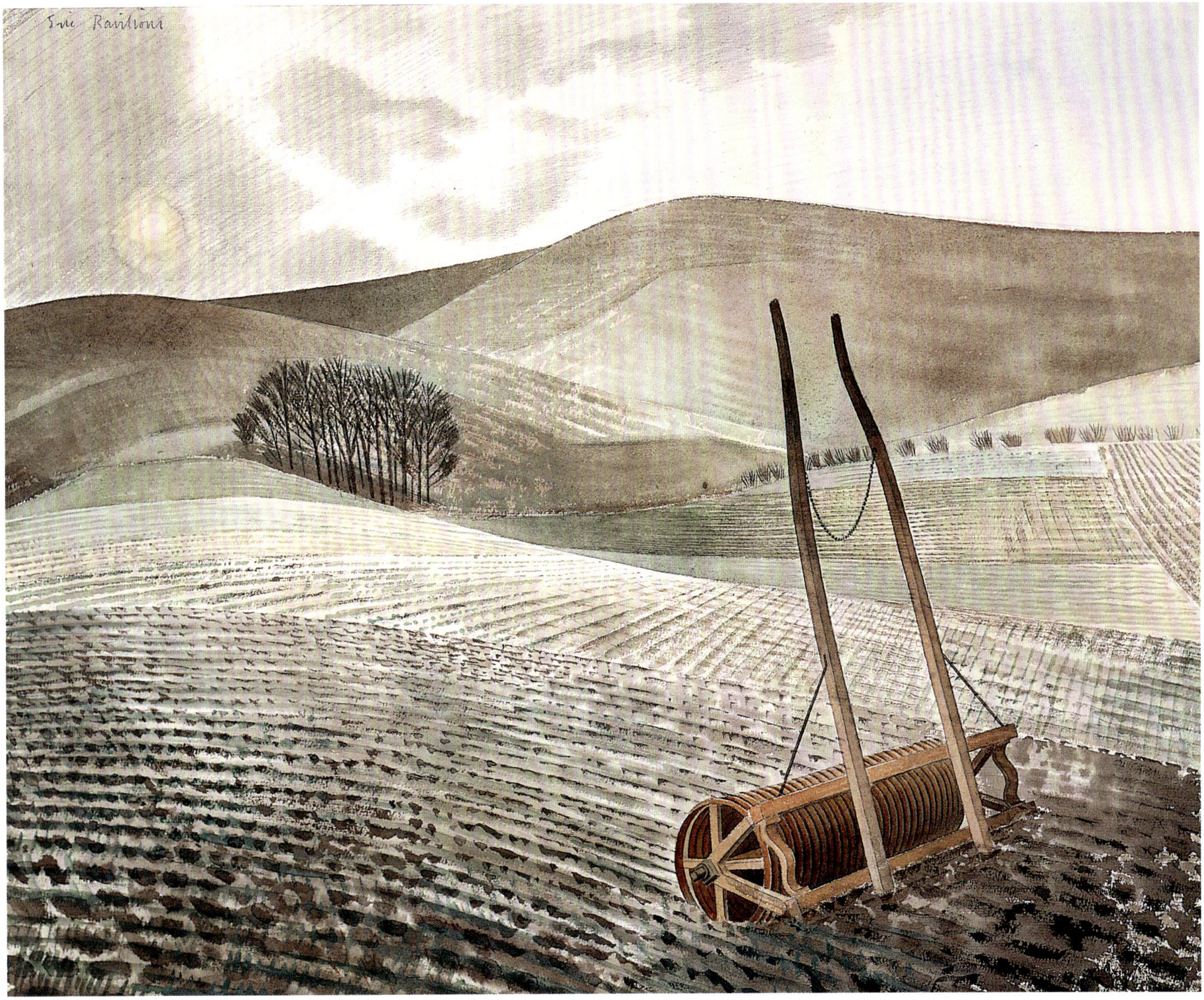

DOWNS IN WINTER

1934, watercolour and pencil, 44.5 × 55.5 cm, Towner, Eastbourne

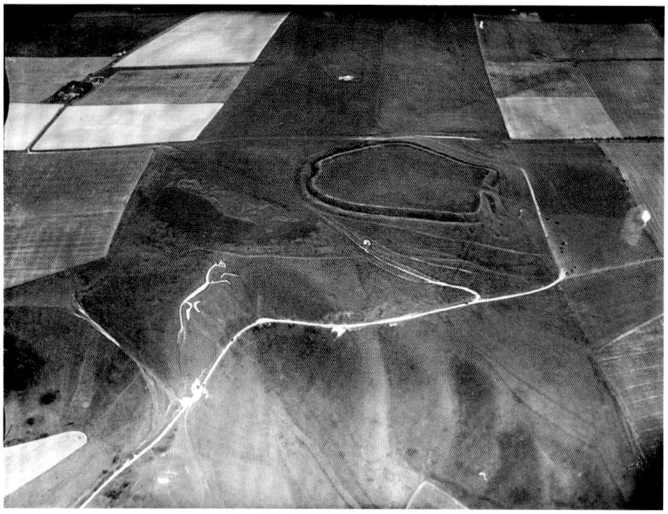

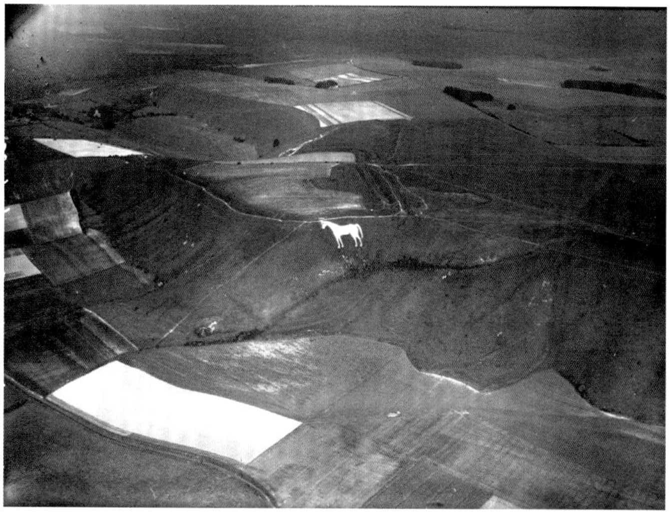

aerial survey, published in book form in 1928 as *Wessex from the Air*. Suddenly it was possible for an amateur archaeologist in Chelsea or Cheltenham to examine ancient monuments in a way unimaginable to Stukeley or Colt-Hoare, and to follow the excavations conducted by William Hawley at Stonehenge and Keiller around Avebury. The Ordnance Survey even published a series of archaeological maps put together by Crawford, which gave a graphic impression of the settlements in use at different times.

But if archaeology was growing more scientific and professional, a powerful romantic streak still persisted. In 1925 Alfred Watkins published *The Old Straight Track: Its Mounds, Beacons, Moats, Sites and Mark Stones* – the book that introduced the idea of ley lines to the world. Crawford refused to accept adverts for it in his journal *Antiquity*. Less controversial but still reliant on imagination rather than science was *Downland Man* (1926), H.J. Massingham's epic work of cultural anthropology. This describes a prehistoric golden age during which a sophisticated Neolithic civilization spread from Egypt and the Middle East across Europe; its English centre was at Avebury, with outposts spread far and wide across the Downs of southern England. Peaceful, scholarly and international in outlook, this was the kind of past that people wanted to embrace in the aftermath of the Great War, and Massingham's theories found a wide audience.

Major George Allen, aerial photographs of Uffington and Westbury white horses, 1933.

Paul Nash, *Landscape of the Megaliths*, lithograph, 1937.

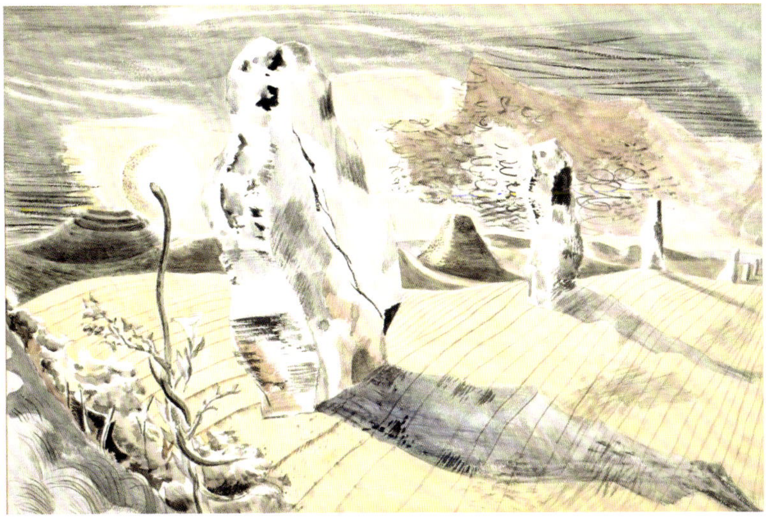

Armed with such volumes, a new generation of motorists and bus-trippers explored the landscape with previously unimaginable freedom. One popular destination was Ivinghoe Beacon, a great hump of chalk overlooking the Vale of Aylesbury close to the meeting point of the Ridgeway and the Icknield Way. In 1929 Paul Nash persuaded someone to drive him to the summit and painted *Wood on the Downs*, a work that conveys perfectly the collision between age-old landscape and modern sensibilities. Against the humped hills, a beech wood rises like a wave – or like the curved wing of a motorcar. 'Millions of motorists must have passed the place', Nash noted wryly when he described the painting. 'It is on the main road on the top of the hill.'

Of course there are no cars in the painting. It was ancient magic Nash sought in the Downs, and though he had painted barbed wire in Flanders he left such modern intrusions out when it came to these differently charged landscapes. Likewise he was not a great fan of archaeology, yet it was probably newspaper reports of Keiller's excavations near Avebury that drew him to the site (by bus) in 1933. The years since *Wood on the Downs* had been passed in a fruitless exploration of abstraction, leading him to wonder publicly whether it was possible to 'go modern', in the sense of conducting formal experiments in art, and still 'be British', remaining true to insular traditions of subject matter and style. In the Avebury megaliths he found inspiration for a series of paintings and prints that

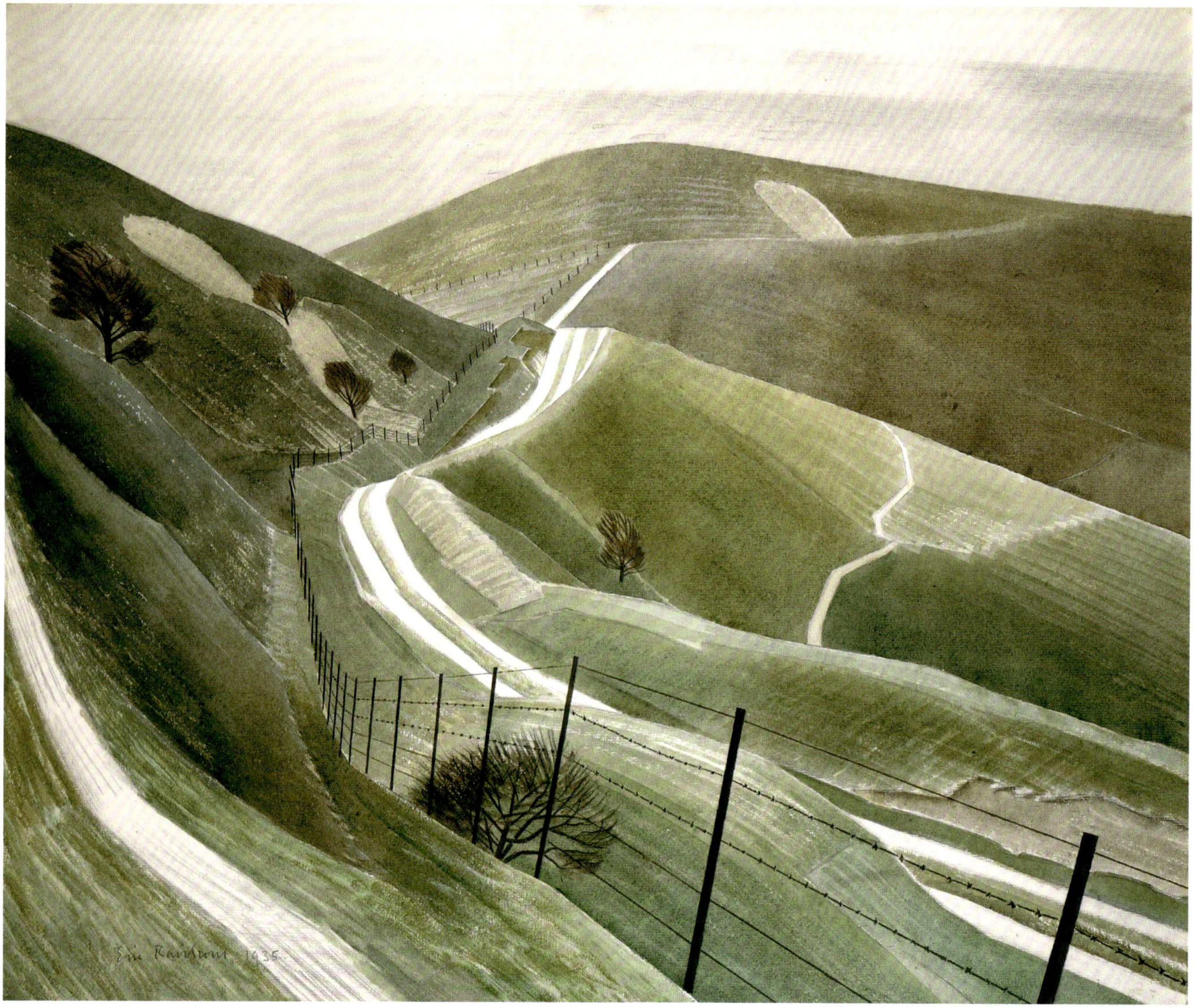

CHALK PATHS

1935, watercolour, 47.0 × 56.5 cm, private collection

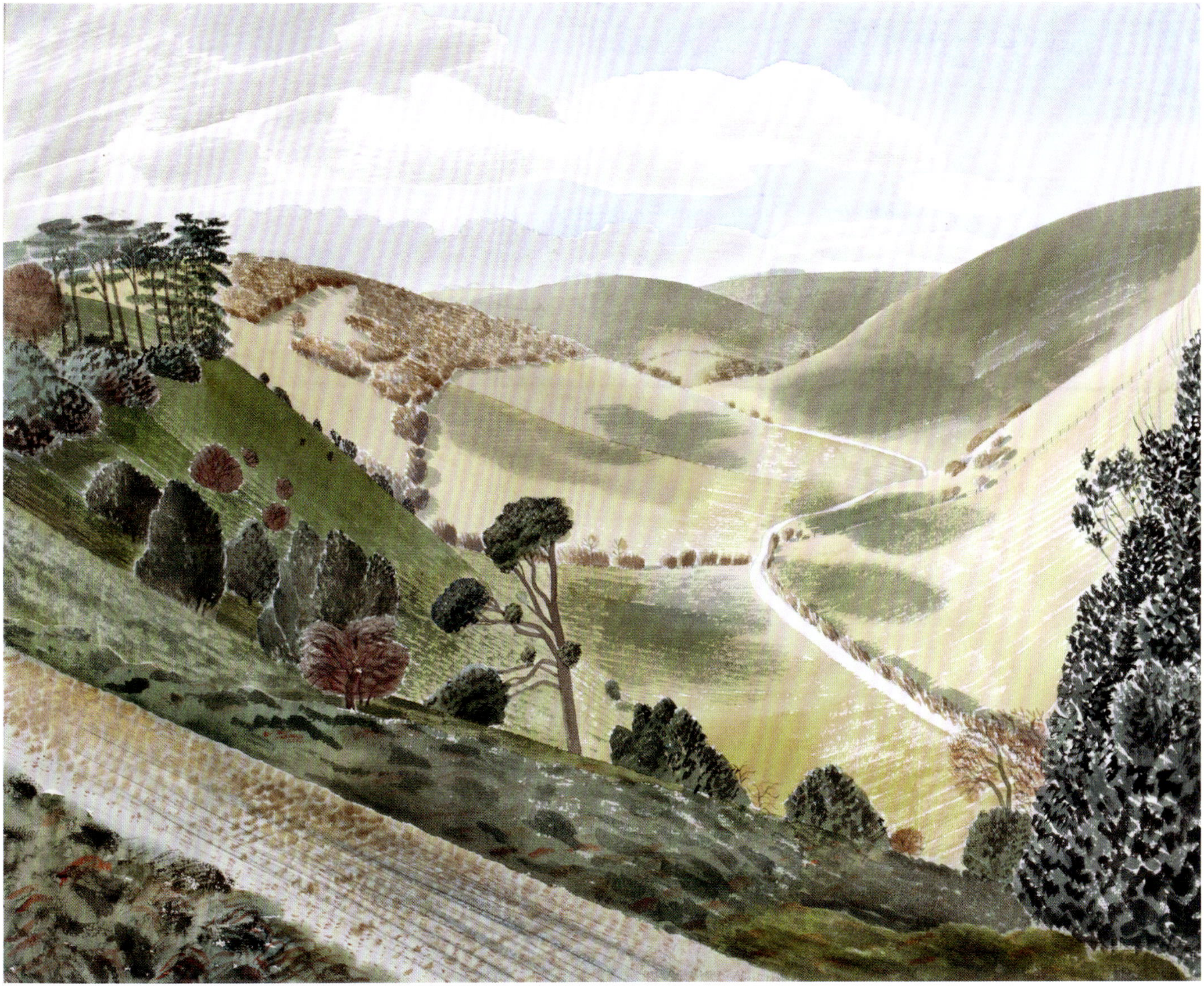

THE CAUSEWAY, WILTSHIRE DOWNS

1937, watercolour and pencil, 44.2 × 55.8 cm, Victoria and Albert Museum

mingle topography and magic, with the strangest of all these being *Event on the Downs*. Painted in 1935, this shows an encounter between a tree root and a ball, two humdrum objects transformed by Nash into 'personages' in an incomprehensible drama. Beyond them a lane leads towards the chalk promontory of Ballard Head, to the east of Swanage.

At the time Nash was living on the Dorset coast and working on a new guidebook to the county. In its advertising the oil company Shell had for several years been exploiting the growing interest in prehistoric sites and similar places of pilgrimage, and now John Betjeman had been put in charge of a new series of Shell Guides. Unusually, these were to be assembled by artists, and in Nash's case this proved astute. Through his watercolours, photographs and words, Dorset came magically alive as a picturesque county where the prehistoric lay just beneath the skin. He was not afraid to express an opinion, writing of Maiden Castle:

> Its presence today, after the immense passage of time, is miraculously undisturbed; the huge contours strike into even the most vulgar mind; the impervious nitwits who climbed on to the megaliths of Stonehenge to be photographed slink out of the shadow of the Maiden uneasily.

Nash didn't mention that in 1934 a vast archaeological excavation had begun at Maiden Castle, led by yet another flamboyant figure, Mortimer Wheeler. At a time when money was tight he exploited popular enthusiasm for his subject. Three years later the dig was still in progress, funded almost entirely by public subscription and with labour provided by an army of youthful volunteers. On summer weekends people walked out from Dorchester to put their penny in the collection bucket.

The Downs and their history were that rare thing, a subject that appealed across boundaries of age and background. At the time you might have read about sites like Maiden Castle not just in *Antiquity* but in the illustrated weekly magazines or the letters pages of *The Times*. Even the avant-garde art magazine *Axis*, a periodical established to champion international abstract art, featured an article by John Piper on *Prehistory from the Air*, which included an aerial photo of the Uffington White Horse.

Meanwhile, Edward Thomas had more readers than he could have imagined, as people looked increasingly to the countryside and in particular to the hills for physical and spiritual regeneration. The Ramblers' Association was founded in 1935, three years after militant walkers led a mass trespass at Kinder Scout, the highest point in the Peak District. Middle-class families abandoned polluted cities to go back to the land, among them a horde of artists, writers and assorted creative types. Never in the history of British art have as many artists explored landscape as they did in the interwar years, and plenty of them travelled the Downs. It's worth noting that the first property bought by the National Trust (in 1896) was Alfriston Clergy House, in the eponymous downland village not far from Eastbourne.

As we have seen, Ravilious knew the chalk hills of Sussex from boyhood, associating this landscape with freedom and adventure. When he went to stay with Peggy Angus at Furlongs he was in his early thirties, a reasonably good teacher and excellent designer who had yet to make his mark as an artist. Furlongs gave him three vital things. First came freedom, with no set meals or rules of any kind to interfere with work, or for that matter intrusive letters from commercial clients. Then the presence of Angus herself, a stern but encouraging taskmaster. And lastly, and most importantly, simplicity. There was no electricity at the cottage and no plumbing. You had to wind a handle ninety-eight times to pull a bucket of water up the well. Mattresses were stuffed with chaff and all the furniture came from junk shops in Lewes.

Step out of the front door and you were in the landscape, with the garden gate the only barrier, and that landscape was also a model of simplicity. Under pale skies filled with that special sea light, the colours were muted and, as Ravilious put it, 'the design so beautifully obvious'. In a burst of activity that began with the cement works pictures, he experienced a personal artistic revolution.

The cement works watercolours are in essence topographical and illustrative: they record his impressions of a place. But the following year, 1935, he produced a pair of watercolours in which a new and distinctive vision is apparent. We have already touched on the first, *Downs in Winter*, but let's take another look. In the foreground the roller is carefully drawn, its handles curving like horns. They are darker towards the tip, creating the illusion that the hills beyond are lighter

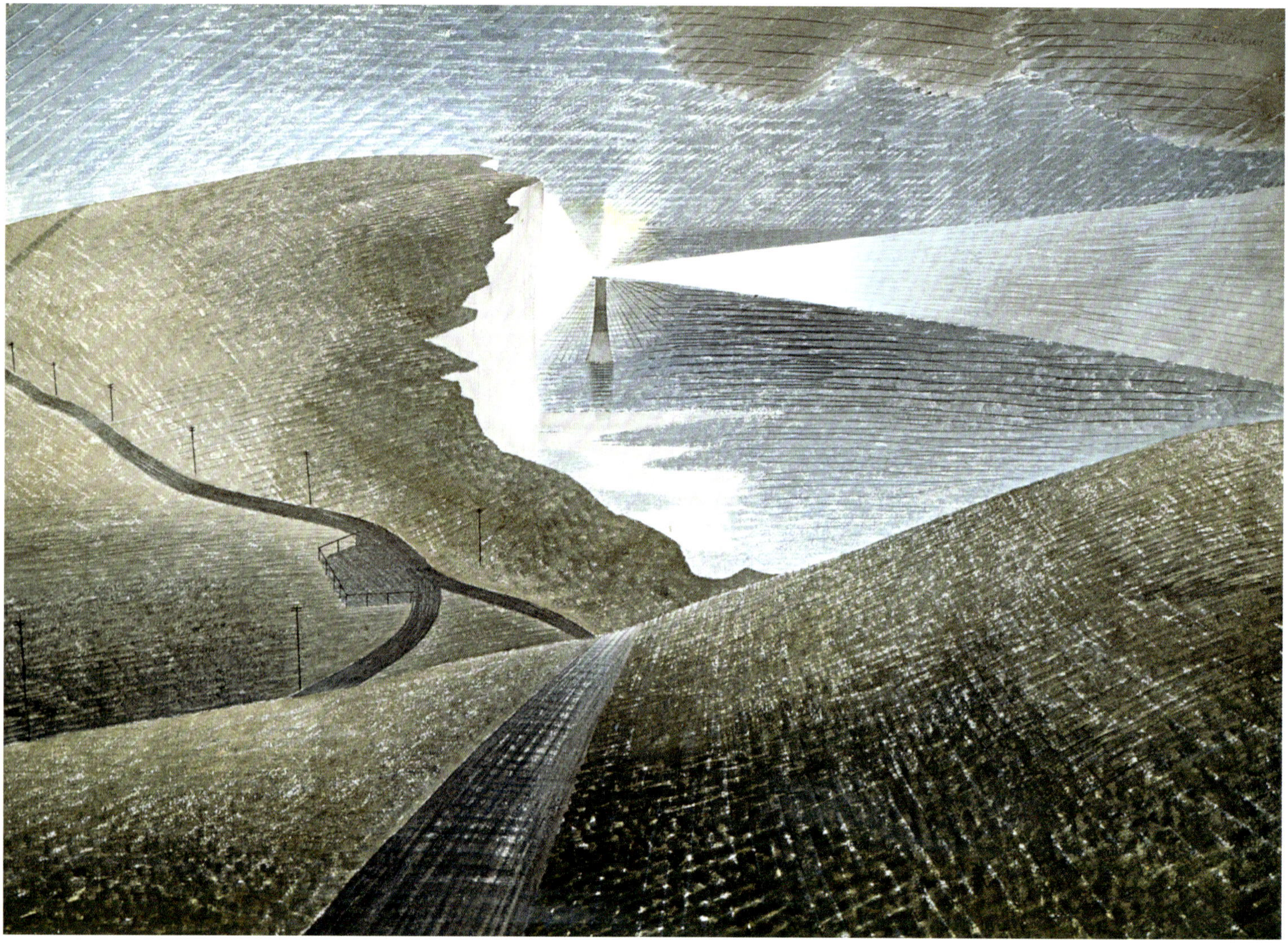

BEACHY HEAD

1939, watercolour and pencil, 57.1 × 72.7 cm, Towner, Eastbourne

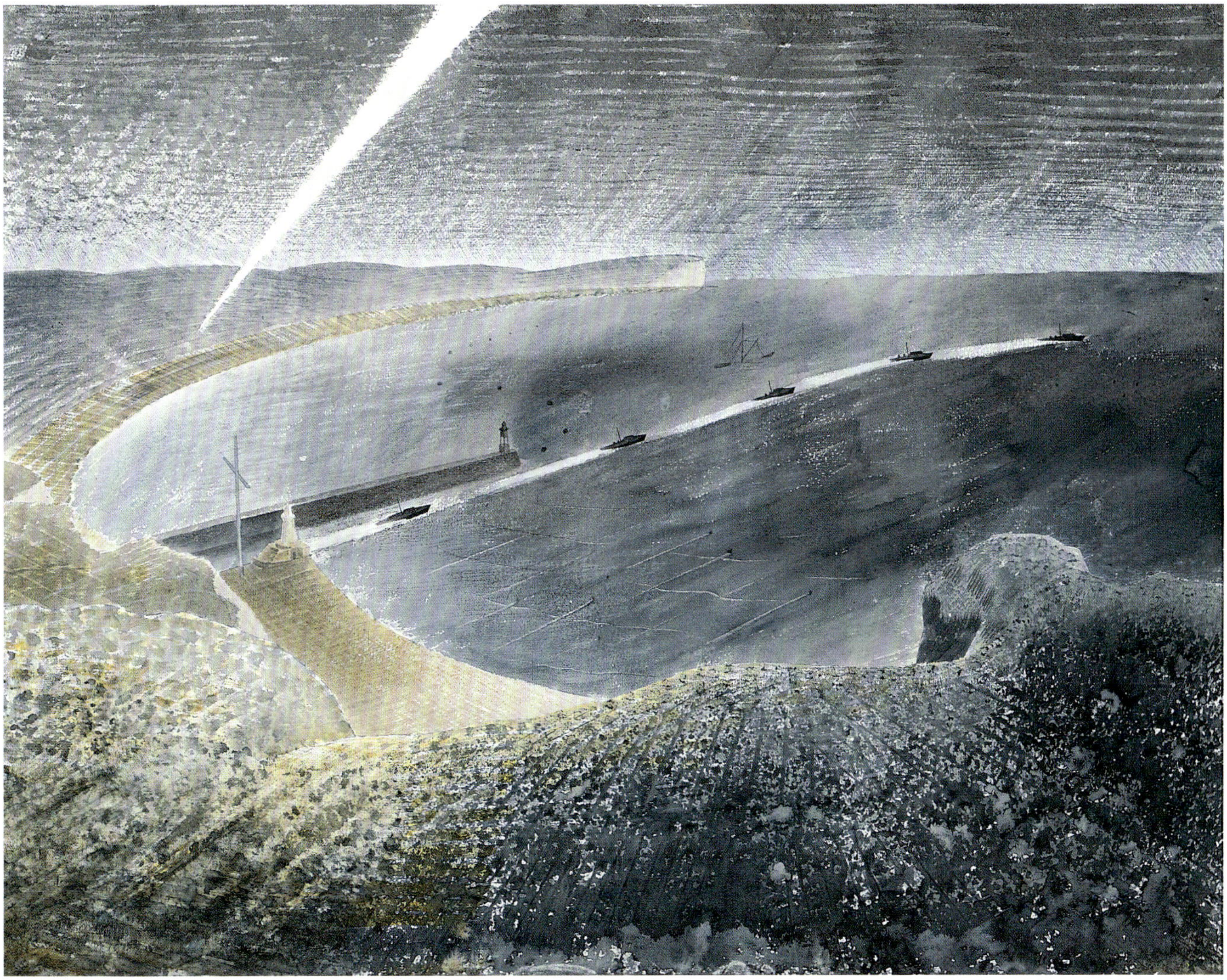

COASTAL DEFENCES

1940, watercolour and pencil, 45.7 × 60.9 cm, Imperial War Museum

towards the summit and so enhancing the feeling of open space. To the left the sun is a pale disc in a hazy sky, its pallor again contrasting with the dark patch of trees below. The rest of the composition relies on a back-and-forth motion of delicately contrasting washes, with the foreground dappled to resemble ploughed land. The whole thing is simple but effective, relying on a subtle geometry that keeps the viewer's gaze moving between roller and copse, while the muted colour scheme and those horn-like handles lend the watercolour just a frisson of mystery. We are in deep time.

Age and modernity are also contrasted to good effect in *Chalk Paths*, a stand-out work of a productive year. Intriguingly – and typically – the watercolour owes its success in part to the inclusion of a modern eyesore. Even today, barbed wire is not much loved, but in the first half of the twentieth century it was perceived as an alien invader, an American invention designed to fence in vast open spaces and quite unsuited to the British countryside. Barbed wire was disliked particularly by the Ramblers Association, whose members sought to open up the rural landscape for recreation. Curiously, though, the fence does not read as a barrier in this composition. Rather it leads the eye deeper into the landscape, along a hillside which is not art-deco smooth but angular and edgy.

There is no room for sentiment here, no softness, yet when Ravilious created this watercolour he was happy and in love. Another twist in the story of his relationship with the Downs lies in the fact that Furlongs in the mid-1930s was the site of regular *rendezvous* with his lover Helen Binyon. The hillside shown here is not far from the cottage, part of a landscape Ravilious once threatened jokingly to map, marking the locations where they had kissed. An artist and puppeteer who had also studied at the Royal College, Helen was the daughter of Great War poet Laurence Binyon, who also happened to be the leading authority on the English watercolour tradition.

In 1933 Binyon wrote approvingly in his survey *English Watercolours* of the modern 'retreat from Impressionism' and 'the new emphasis of solidity and stability, the hatred of all softness'. The picturesque was still alive and well, meanwhile, but it 'has changed its nature, the place of ruined castle and tumble-down cottage being taken by steam-crane and gasometer'.

These, though, had already acquired the veneer of age by the 1930s, whereas Ravilious was equally interested in man-made things that were brand new, like the waterwheel installed up the lane from Furlongs and still discernible today amid the undergrowth. This appetite for the new stood him in good stead when he was awarded his first contract as a war artist at the beginning of 1940, since he found himself tasked with recording a war of machines. Given the job of portraying coastal defences, he spent the autumn of 1940 scrambling around Newhaven Fort in a tin hat, watching German aircraft fly as they pleased overhead. His watercolour of patrol boats heading seaward at night echoes one of his most brilliant peacetime works, *Beachy Head*, which is in turn reminiscent of Richard Nevinson's Great War paintings of searchlight beams.

The following autumn Ravilious was sent to Dover, where he found much to stimulate him. This was, after all, the front line, with bunkers and tunnels dug into the chalk. On both sides of the Channel massive guns were perpetually engaged in a slow-moving duel, and if firing started at night he would jump out of bed and rush up the hill from his digs, hoping to capture the fleeting spectacle of distant explosions. *Bombing the Channel Ports* has a similar theme, while also featuring the kind of unusual man-made object Ravilious loved. Just to the right of centre you can see on the cliff edge a wedge of concrete, in fact an acoustic mirror designed to pick up and amplify the sound of approaching enemy aircraft. Such structures were built around the south coast during and after the Great War, but by 1941 they had been superseded by radar. Ravilious may well have chosen this vantage point so he could include this piece of obsolete technology.

Not long afterwards Ravilious left the Royal Navy for the RAF, and in August 1942 flew to Iceland. He had only been there a couple of days when he volunteered for a rescue mission, only for his plane to be lost. He was thirty-nine.

There is little point in wondering what Ravilious would have done next, except that he might, in the right circumstances, have gone back to the *White Horse* dummy and created his book of chalk figures and ancient monuments. The idea had been suggested to him in the autumn of 1939 by Noel Carrington, publisher of Ravilious's 1938 book *High Street*. Carrington had worked out that if an artist could be persuaded to design, illustrate and (preferably) write a

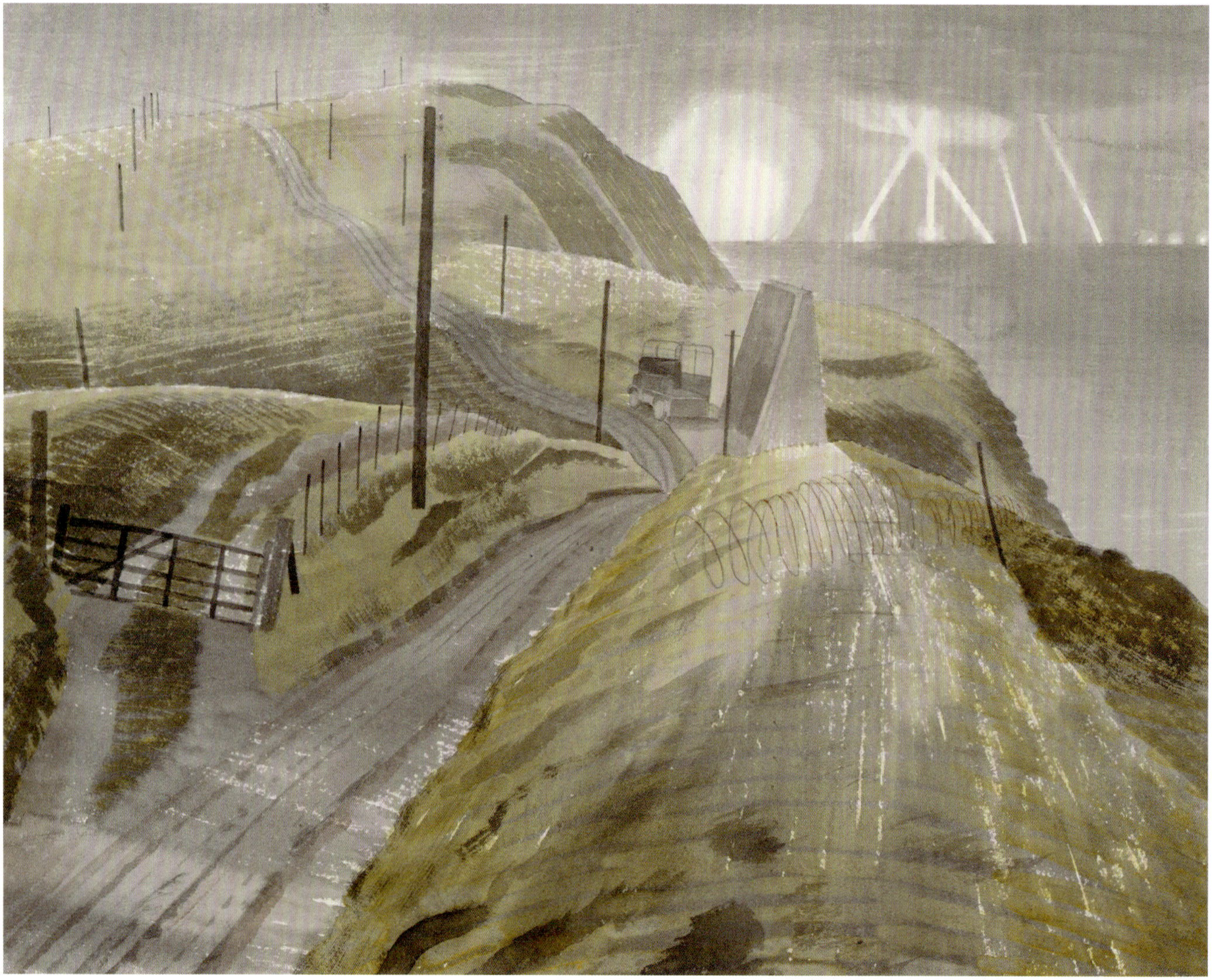

BOMBING THE CHANNEL PORTS

1941, watercolour and pencil, 38.7 × 48.8 cm, Imperial War Museum

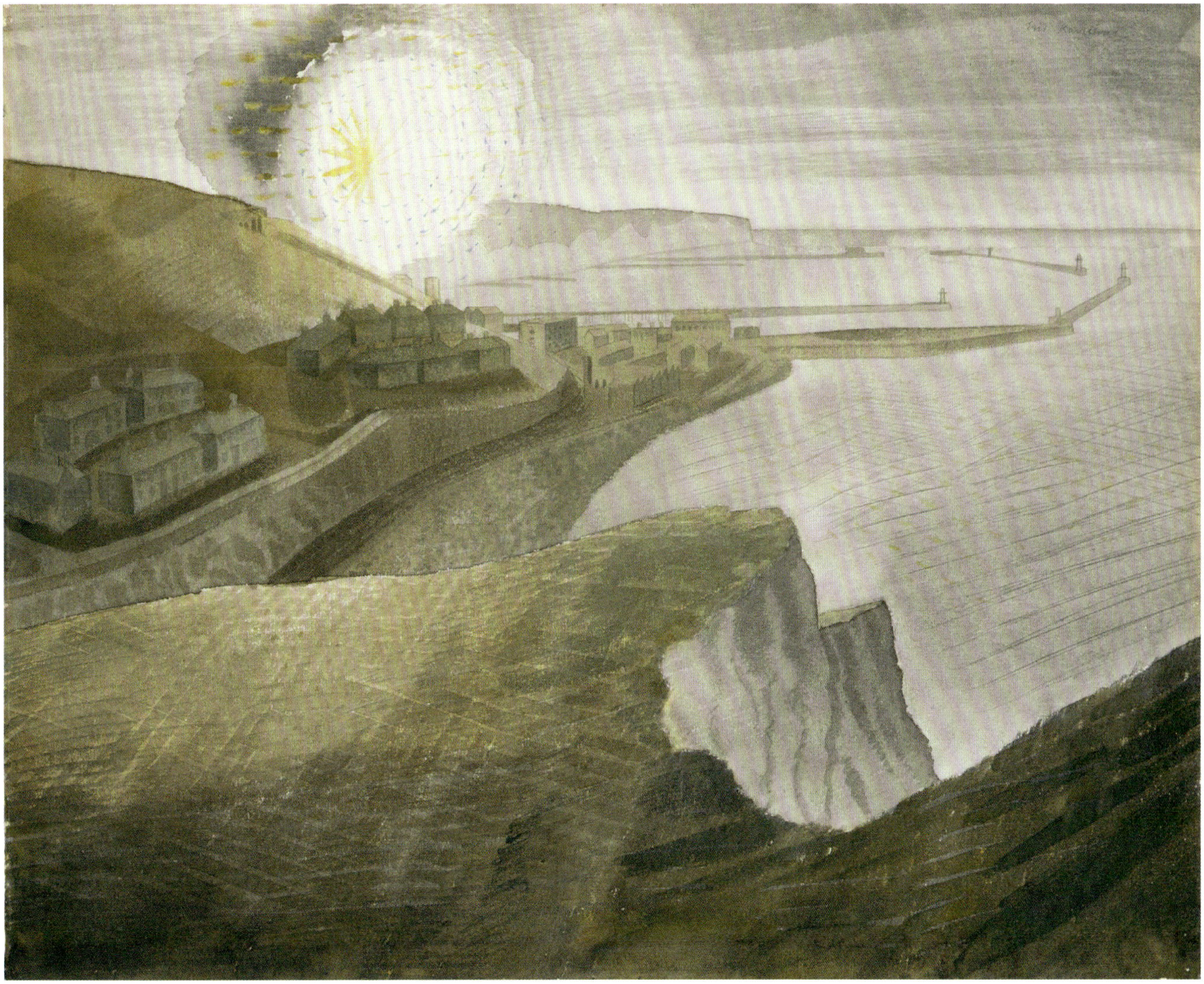

SHELLING BY NIGHT

1941, watercolour and pencil, 44.5 × 54.6 cm, Tate

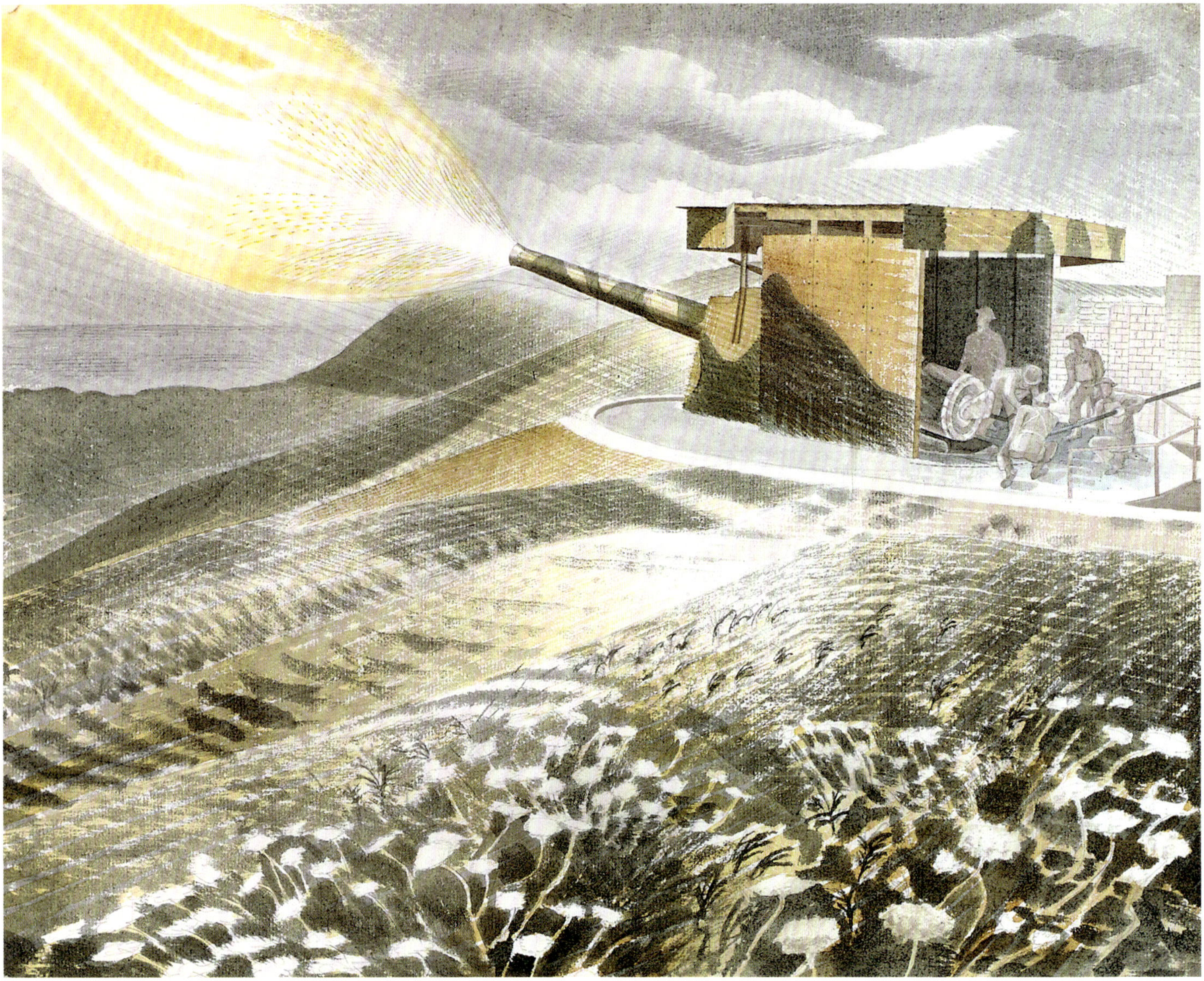

FIRING A 9.2 GUN

1941, watercolour and pencil, 41.2 × 52.7 cm, Imperial War Museum

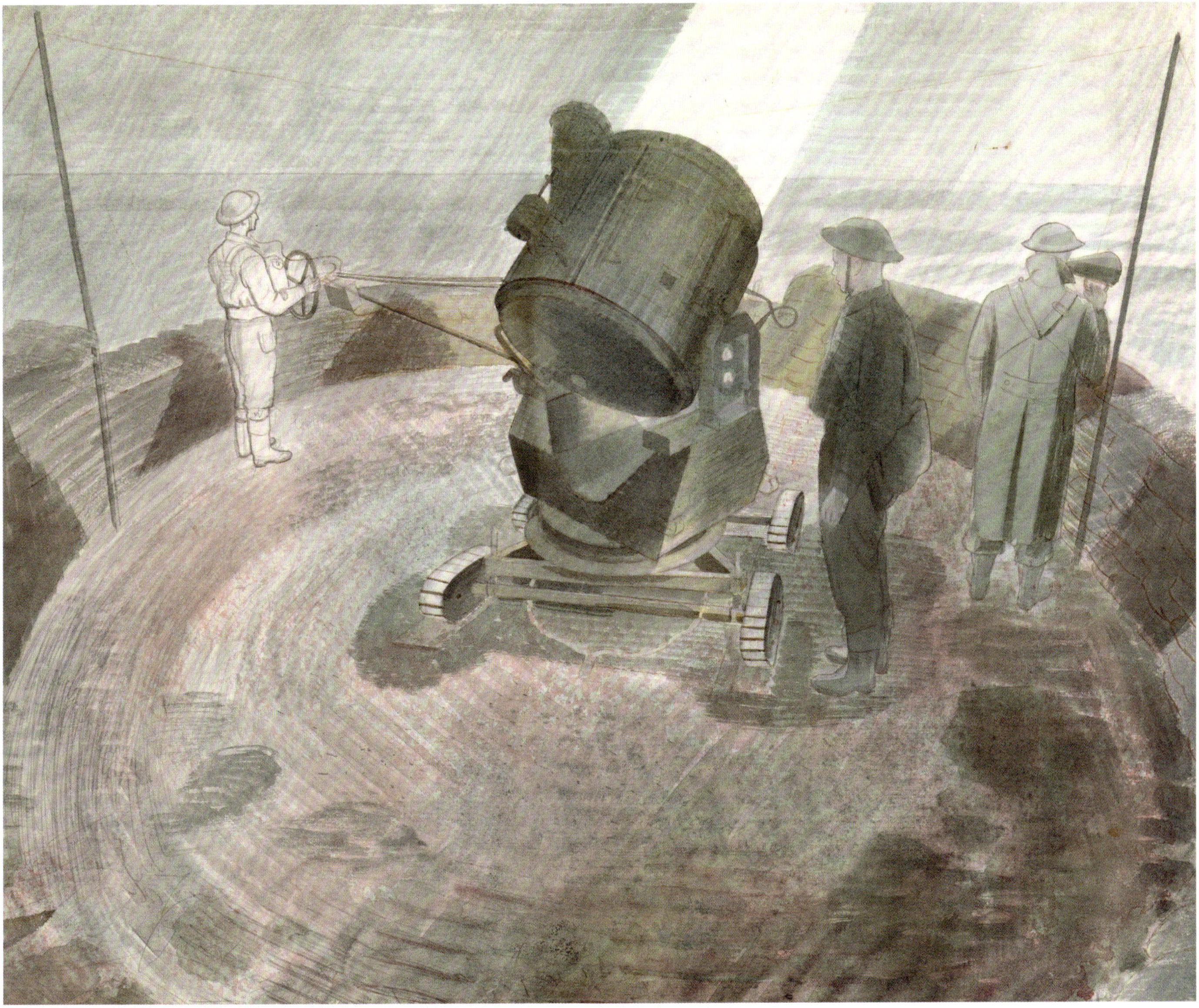

COASTAL DEFENCES, SEARCHLIGHT AND CREW

1941, watercolour and pencil, 43.8 × 53.6 cm, Imperial War Museum

children's book, working directly on the lithographic plates used for printing, the book could be produced very cheaply. The idea came from the Soviet Union, where in the 1920s Lenin's determination to educate a vast illiterate population saw illustrated books produced for pennies and printed in millions.

Unfortunately it wasn't until the outbreak of war that Carrington got the green light from Penguin Books for the series. The choice of chalk figures and hill forts was a pretty obvious one given public interest in the subject, and when he approached Ravilious he received an enthusiastic response – unsurprisingly, given that all other art work had dried up and nothing definite had come through about the rumoured war artist scheme. Ravilious had not spent much time in the southern hills since that *annus mirabilis* at Furlongs, but in 1937 a painting trip with John Nash produced the sublime *Causeway, Wiltshire Downs*. Then came another breakthrough work…

In May 1939 Ravilious held his third solo exhibition, at the London gallery of Tooth & Sons. It was a startling success. Writing in *The Times*, Eric Newton declared that it was almost impossible to describe in words what Ravilious had achieved in his watercolours, except that 'he makes you feel that each object matters immensely… I can honestly say that I had never realised the wiriness of wire netting before looking at his *Cliffs in March*' (a Sussex picture, now lost). Other critics shared Newton's delight and bafflement, and when Ravilious returned to Furlongs that August – his first proper stay in four years – he set to work with renewed confidence. He painted watercolours of the cottage, inside and out, before returning to visit a familiar friend: the Wilmington Giant.

His watercolour of this tantalizing chalk figure is masterly. Glance across the paper, first of all, and you notice that every inch has been carefully worked to lend variety to sky and land. Positioned just left and above the centre of the composition, the Giant seems ready to pivot on one of those strange staves and come walking towards us along the line suggested by the curve of fence. The stand of corn to the left, a symbol of summer, attracts our eye to the foreground before the fence takes it back to the Giant's feet. But it is the fence itself that steals the scene, with that dark post looming over everything and then those delicate trails of wire. No one who has studied this watercolour carefully will ever look at barbed wire in quite the same way again.

Once the picture was finished it was snapped up by the V&A. Did Carrington see the watercolour, or perhaps a photo of it, and immediately understand the possibilities? By now Ravilious was employed as an observer of aircraft on the hill above his home in Castle Hedingham, Essex, but in December he abruptly rushed off on a whistlestop tour of chalk figures. In a few days he visited Weymouth (to draw the figure of George III on horseback) and Cerne Abbas (for that other, less modest, Giant), before travelling north to record his impressions of the white horses at Westbury and Uffington. How he did all this as a non-driver in wartime is a mystery, but by the time he went off to begin his first contract as a war artist in February he had completed the stunning set of watercolours that were to form the basis of *White Horse*.

If we look at *The Westbury Horse* and *The Vale of the White Horse* we quickly see how remarkable a watercolourist Ravilious had become. Even now he was regularly visiting the print rooms of London's museums to study past masters, and often borrowed compositional ideas from artists like William Pars or John Robert Cozens. There are echoes of the past in these works, but they are not old-fashioned or nostalgic. They are rigorous. In each case the hillside is almost tangibly three-dimensional. A close friend of Henry Moore, he had been to see the sculptor's *Reclining Figure* on the terrace at Bentley Wood, Serge Chermayeff's modernist house near Lewes. Moore intended the sculpture to be viewed in the landscape; Ravilious has turned the landscape into sculpture.

When it came to portraying the two-dimensional chalk figures on this 3D ground he drew on another area of his experience: designing for Wedgwood. Other than in terms of scale there's not such a great difference between a design invented for the rounded side of a teapot and a chalk figure carved into a hill. Yet although there's undoubtedly something domestic and decorative about these pictures, they still radiate a strong sense of place and climate. While a train steaming across the plain adds a sense of scale and grandeur to the Westbury horse, the Uffington horse is shown under heavy rain, in wild grassland. This is as it should be, since the former could be seen as a blown-up version of a Georgian heraldic device, while the latter belongs to a past too remote for us to know. Strictly speaking only giants can see the full outline of the Uffington horse from the ground, so Ravilious presumably referred to aerial photos.

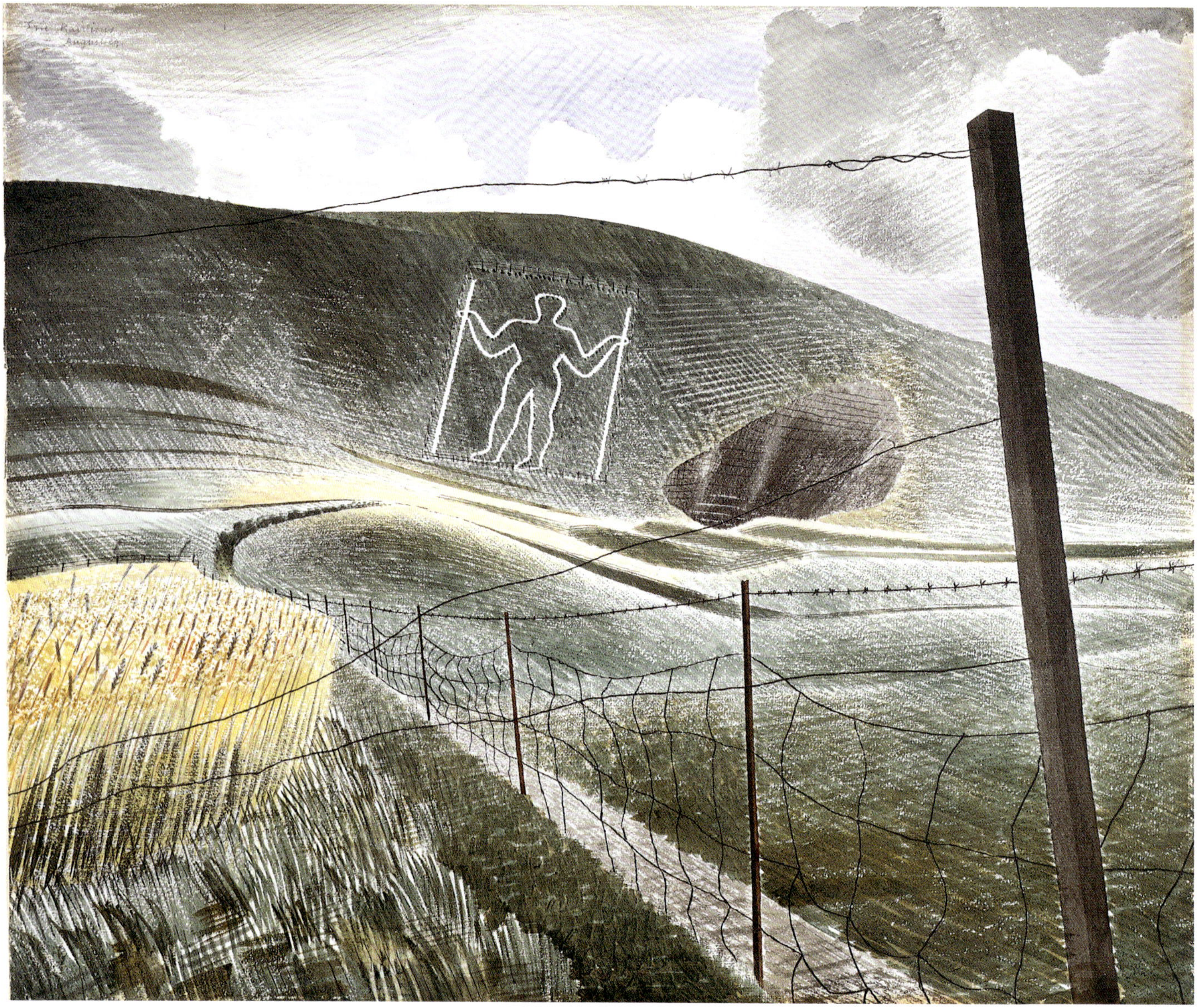

THE WILMINGTON GIANT

1939, watercolour and pencil, 44.7 × 53.7 cm, Victoria and Albert Museum

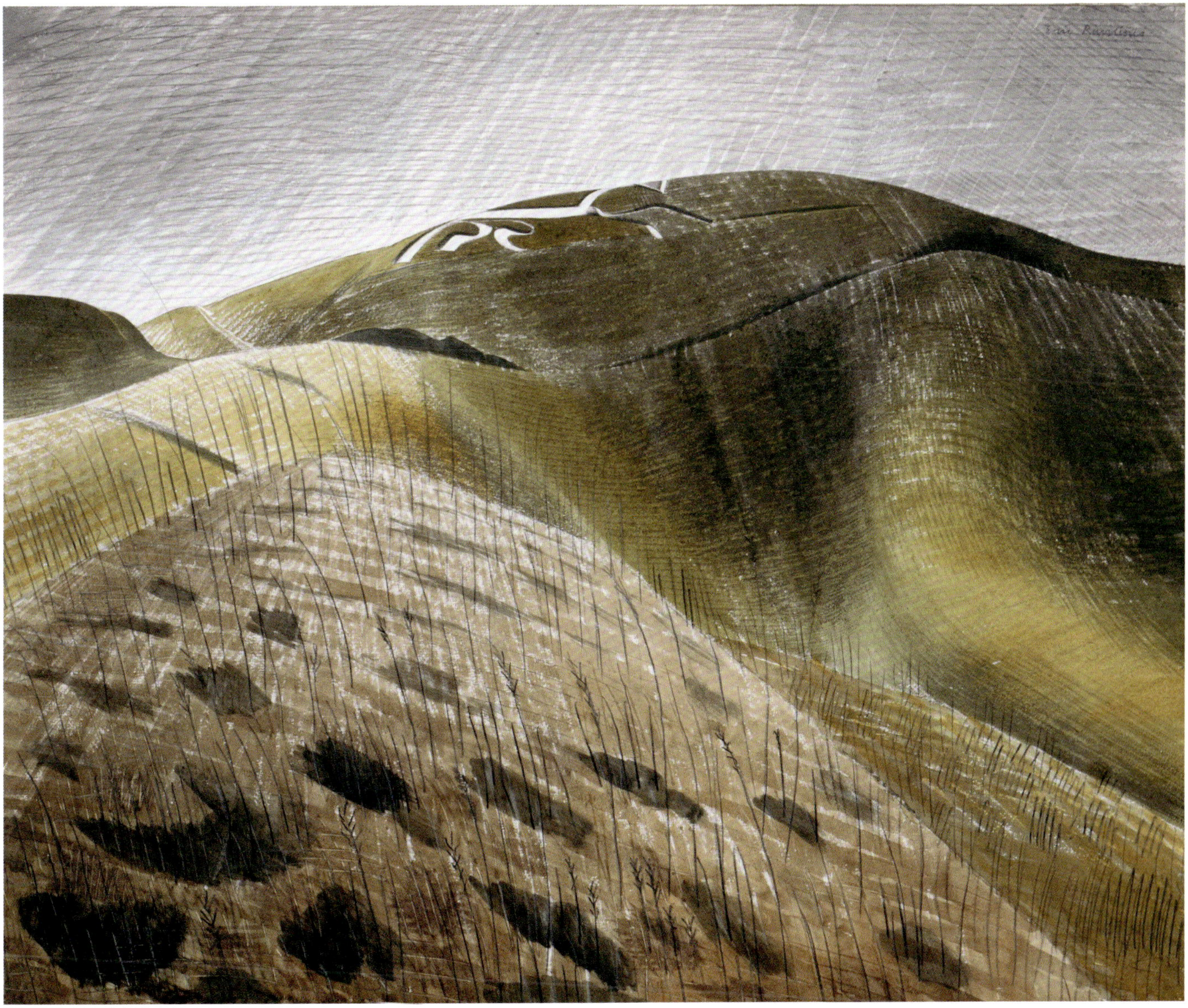

THE VALE OF THE WHITE HORSE

c.1939, watercolour and pencil, 45.1 × 55.2 cm, Tate

Once again we see the dance of the prehistoric and the modern. The mania for archaeology and for mass exploration of the Downs in the 1930s were modern phenomena, and Ravilious was as much a modern artist as Henry Moore. Lithography was a modern invention, as was the paperback book, and there would have been no Picture Puffins without Lenin. A few months after Ravilious completed these watercolours the Nazis unleashed *Blitzkrieg* – their new and terrifying form of warfare – on western Europe. As the Luftwaffe invaded the skies of southern England the chalk figures were hastily covered over in a bid to deter enemy navigators, an activity Ravilious briefly considered as a subject. They were still hidden when the artist was lost, in the most northerly theatre of a global war.

Ravilious left behind Tirzah and three young children: John, James and Anne. Sixty years later, to mark her father's centenary, Anne co-edited a book devoted to his work as a war artist, accompanied by a selection of his correspondence. Included among the letters was one written to Ravilious by Noel Carrington. It is dated 29 January 1941. He writes:

> Thanks for the Puffin dummy. I am glad to see that you have agreed to put in earthworks and castles. That suggests to me the title of 'Downland Man' which would not exclude later downland figures. I believe we could get someone like Massingham to do a very simple text giving the children some idea of how downland man lived and we might have a few drawings of the implements that have been found in the barrows and earth works. The pictorial emphasis would remain on the chalk figures and some of the castles.

His letter ends with a promise: 'I will take great care of the Whitehorse dummy.' So Ravilious did not take the dummy with him to Iceland. In fact Carrington kept it until the 1950s when he moved office, at which point he gave it to artist Roland Collins. Unaware of its status as a lost relic, Collins looked after the fragile artefact until 2012, when he put it up for auction.

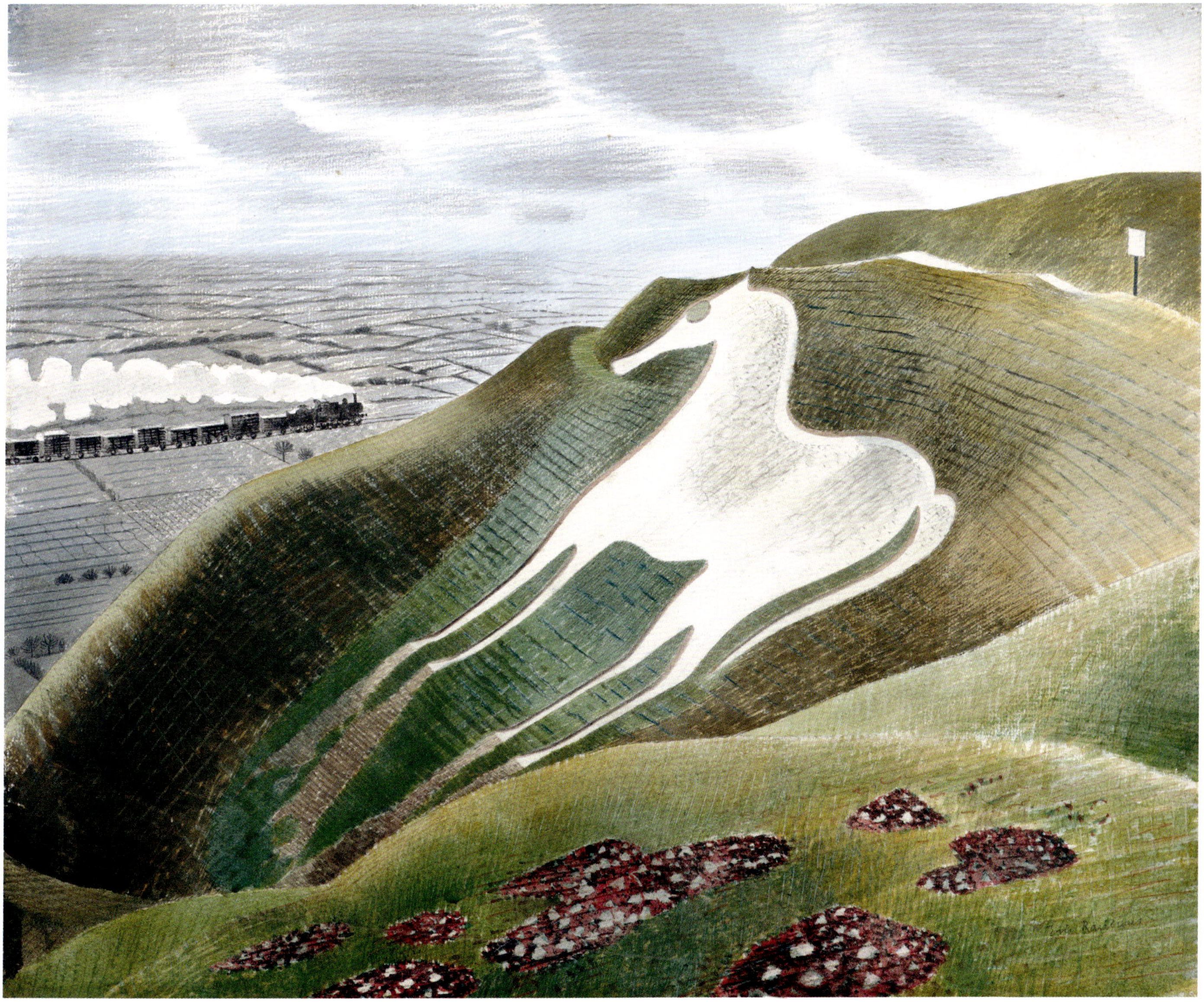

THE WESTBURY HORSE

1939, watercolour and pencil, 44.4 × 54.6 cm, private collection
on loan to Towner, Eastbourne

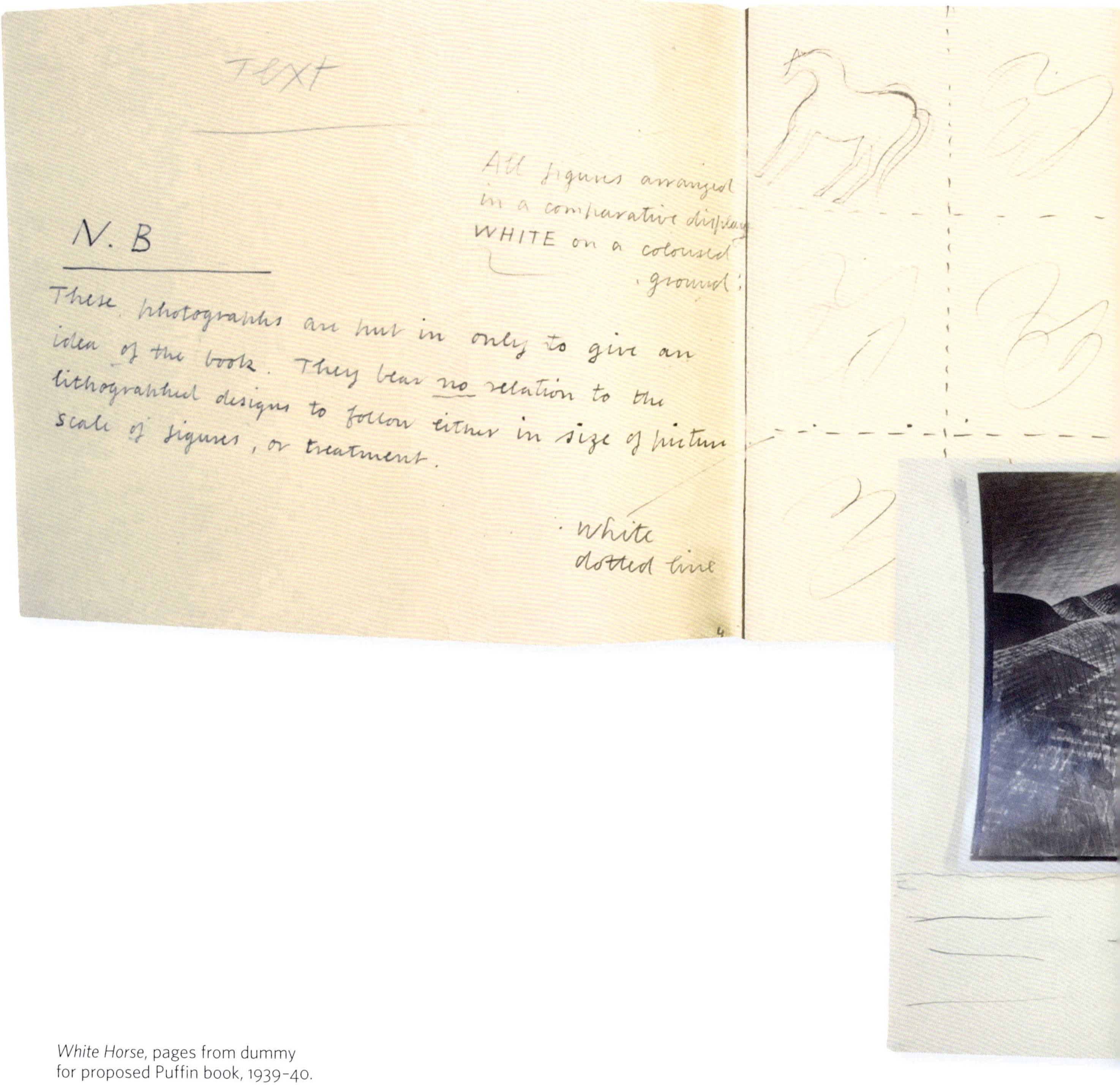

White Horse, pages from dummy for proposed Puffin book, 1939–40.

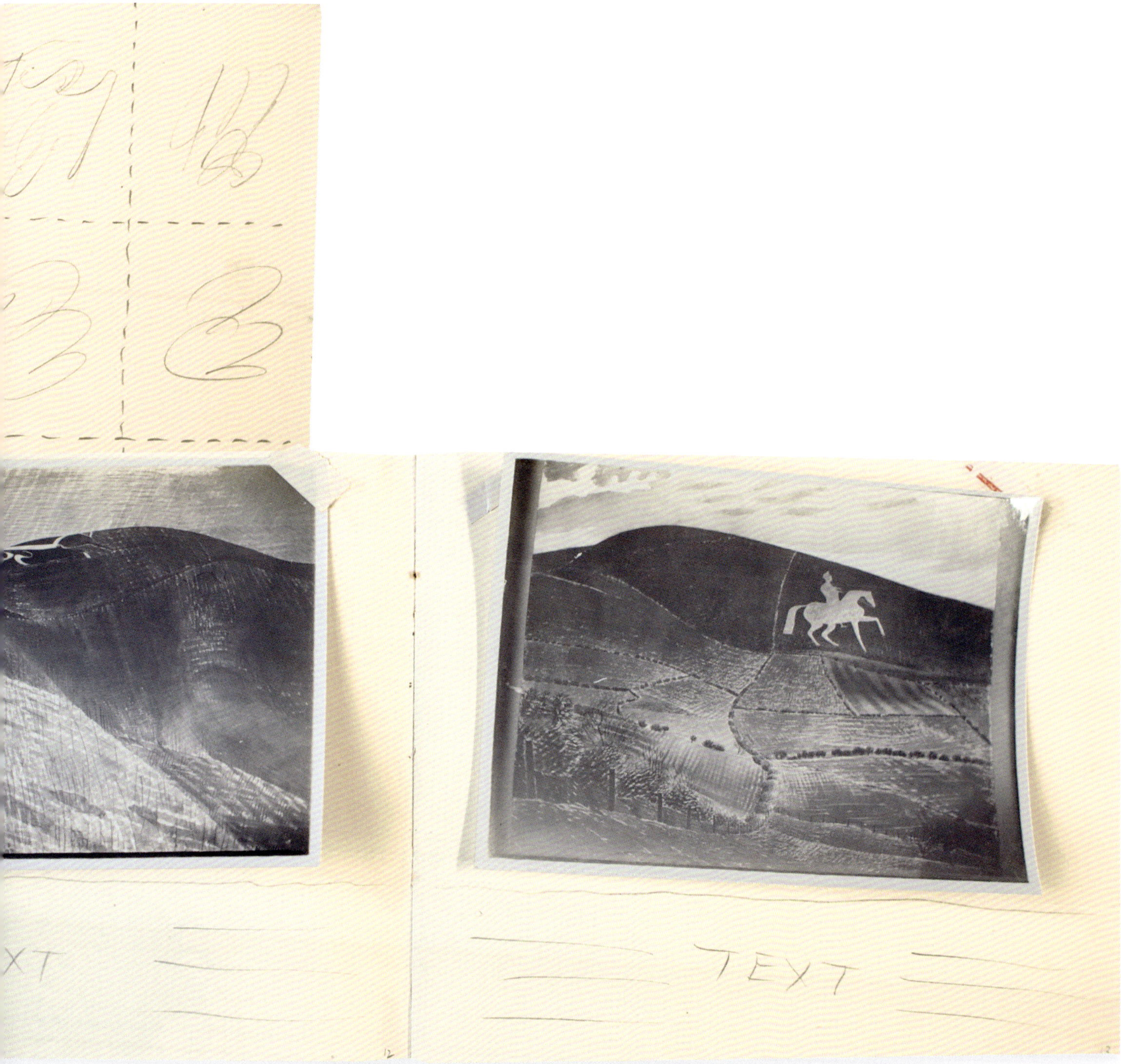
TEXT

ACKNOWLEDGEMENTS

Lenders
Amgueddfa Cymru – National Museum Wales
British Museum
East Sussex Brighton & Hove Record Office
IWM (Imperial War Museums)
Private collections
Tate
Towner, Eastbourne
Victoria and Albert Museum, London

Funders
The Weston Loan Programme with Art Fund
The Arts Council National Lottery Projects
National Lottery Heritage Fund
Mercers' Company
South Downs National Parks Authority
The Golsoncott Foundation
Verdon-Smith Family Charitable Settlement
The Walter Guinness Charitable Trust
and numerous individual donations

Exhibition sponsored by
Gaiger Construction and Development
Wansbroughs Solicitors

With thanks to
The exhibition was made possible as a result of the Government Indemnity Scheme. The Wiltshire Museum would like to thank HM Government for providing Government Indemnity and the Department for Digital, Culture, Media and Sport and Arts Council England for arranging the indemnity.

Catalogue sponsored by
Mr Julian Francis

Image credits
p. 24, image © Ashmolean Museum, University of Oxford. pp. 14, 35, photo: Tate. pp. 27, 40, © Victoria and Albert Museum, London. p. 19, © Amgueddfa Cymru – National Museum of Wales. pp. 9, 11, 12, 13, 18, 23, 30, 43, image Towner, Eastbourne. p. 10 © The Trustees of the British Museum. pp. 31, 34, 36, 37, © Imperial War Museum. p. 26, image © private collection/Bridgeman Images. pp. 14, 22, image © private collection.

Wiltshire Museum Team
Heather Ault, Lisa Brown, David Dawson, Mandy Dixon, Amy Hammett, Rachael Holtom, Karen Jones, Ali Rushent, Jane Schön, Emma Sykes, Nicola Trowell

INDEX OF WORKS

James Russell would like to thank David Dawson for commissioning the exhibition and for his invaluable archaeological expertise. Thank you to staff at Wiltshire Museum for persevering in difficult times, particularly Heather Ault and Karen Jones, and to Lucy Morton for a fabulous design. Thank you to all the lenders, corporate and private, for allowing us to reschedule the exhibition in the face of Covid: not a single work was lost. For their support and help thank you to Neil Jennings, Karen Taylor and Julian Francis and to Tim Mainstone, Dayna Stevens and Miranda and Ollie Russell, fellow explorers of the downland scene. Finally, James would like to thank Anne Ullmann and her late husband Louis, to whom this catalogue is dedicated.

Published to accompany the exhibition

Eric Ravilious: Downland Man

25 September 2021–30 January 2022
Wiltshire Museum, Devizes

www.wiltshiremuseum.org.uk

Registered charity no. 1080096

Published by the Wiltshire Archaeological
and Natural History Society
41 Long Street
Devizes SN10 1NS

ISBN 978-0-947723-17-0

Designed and typeset in Perpetua by illuminati, Grosmont
Printed and bound in Wales by Gomer Press Limited